THE COFFEE HOUSE MINISTRY

The Coffee House Ministry

by John D. Perry, Jr.

Foreword by
Malcolm Boyd

JOHN KNOX PRESS
Richmond, Virginia

Third printing 1967

Grateful acknowledgment is made to the Coffee Information Service and the Pan-American Coffee Bureau for their permission to use photographs and recipes. Other photographs used by courtesy of the Chicago Sun-Times, the Des Moines Tribune and Register, and Malcolm Boyd. Much of the material in Chapter One originally appeared in *motive* magazine under the title "Evangelism or Evasion?"

LIBRARY OF CONGRESS CATALOG CARD NUMBER: 66-17597

PRINTED IN THE UNITED STATES OF AMERICA
29-1491

CONTENTS

THE COFFEE HOUSE MINISTRY

ACKNOWLEDGMENTS

When I was a junior at Yale Divinity School and directing "Koinonia" coffee house at the University of Connecticut on weekends, I was thwarted by the absence of written materials about the coffee house ministry movement. Under the guidance and encouragement of G. Parker Rossman, Professor of Campus Ministry, I conducted a rudimentary mail-order survey of campus-oriented coffee houses for a class term paper. Thanks to his continued support and helpful criticism, a summary report was prepared for *The Christian Century* (February 10, 1965), and a theological essay on coffee house evangelism for *motive* magazine (March 1965).

Thanks are also due to Warren Lane Molton, who, as Director of the University Christian Fellowship at the University of Connecticut, supervised my coffee house ministry there.

Warren W. Ost, Director of the National Council of Churches' Commission on Christian Ministry with People in Leisure-Recreation, deserves the credit for making me aware of the widespread interest in coffee house ministries, beyond the confines of the academic community. He provided several opportunities for me to meet with National Council of Churches and denominational officials to discuss the movement.

The present book is richer by far through the generosity of the National Coffee Association, which made available to the National Council of Churches a $5,000 grant to finance the "Coffee House Study Project" under Mr. Ost's supervision, during July and August of 1965. For that project, my wife and I visited some thirty coffee houses from New York City to Los Angeles, and I corresponded with almost two hundred more. The local coffee house managers and chairmen who took time to welcome us and share their programs and plans deserve and have our appreciation.

Malcolm Boyd deserves my thanks, both for his continued helpful criticism throughout my studies of the movement, and for preparing the foreword to this volume. My appreciation is extended to Mrs. Malcolm Davis, who patiently and carefully prepared the manuscript. Mrs. Harriett P. Pitt of the Coffee Information Service has provided a great deal of information and assistance.

But my greatest appreciation is reserved for my wife Carolyn. As my fiancée and an undergraduate at the University of Connecticut, she held together my first venture in the coffee house ministry movement by her able work as kitchen chairman. She has patiently followed me in my pursuit of the movement, typing various manuscripts, listening at interviews, and criticizing everything as only she can.

John D. Perry, Jr.
Burlington, Vermont

FOREWORD BY MALCOLM BOYD

The coffee house has outlasted mere vogue and is a permanent part of the cultural scene, as this engaging and deeply serious book tells us. In fact, the coffee house is now an accepted reality in the church's ministry as the contemporary church strives to move out from its incestuous preoccupation with self into the world of real men and women. It is in the arena of the world, and to these men and women, that the gospel is to be proclaimed.

So far, so good. Words dealing with "evangelism" and "the theology of the laity" are conjured up, and one is delighted because theology is being seized by its vestment-heavy neck and forced outside ridiculously immature churchly settings. Yet there is a new peril. This new movement has a suggestion of preciosity, smacks of the romantic, and might even become the old incestuous preoccupation with self, this time disguised as mission.

How can we tell? The criterion of the church-related coffee house's integrity can be found in its encounter with the world. Does it, even while prating about God's concern and love for the world, shy away from that same world God created and redeemed? How neurotic, or healthy, is the coffee house in its contemplation of those bizarre scyllas, the "sacred" and the "secular"?

Indeed, how self-righteous is the coffee house concerning its appointment of missionary? It will either be playing church by candlelight—and talking to itself, amid clever new surroundings—or else be involved in real concerns outside its parochial contexts. It will become fundamentally a p.r.-motivated gimmick—a fate which also confronts the proliferation of "jazz masses" and "folk masses"—or else a sober, quite serious contemporary expression of the church's evangelism and, therefore, its duty.

I recall my first visit to *any* coffee house. It was new, startlingly honest, and I loved it. I found I could speak in a coffee house, informally and about any number of subjects, for a couple of hours; people would be sprawled on the floor, someone reading by a small lamp, someone else sitting close by a date; and there was no bourgeois "time limit" or even an implicitly accepted limit on the kind of subject matter or material used. Inside a church, on the other hand, both limits would be strictly observed. Too, in the coffee house there was talk-back and an experience of participation which seemed like fresh air. Later, five plays which I wrote about race relations would be given their initial performances inside coffee house theatres, afterward also to be presented in church sanctuaries.

Yes, I got in trouble meddling with this "new" form of evangelism. So—always and inevitably—do numbers of Christians, regardless of what "new" forms which are currently labeled avant-garde but are, of course, apostolically as old as the hills. In my own case, a church authority, writing in his diocesan journal, drew a picture of "beatniks" and irregularities inside coffee houses. He scored "the puny minds of modern intellectuals" and, unmistakably pointing a finger at my coffee house activities, wrote: "You can't think of yourself as a beloved son of God and at the same time go around with matted hair, dirty bodies and black underwear. I think that of these three probably the black underwear is the least objectionable." In the ensuing controversy—during which time I resigned my chaplaincy in protest against what I felt was heretical in the profoundest sense—I acquired a new label when a New York newspaper headline-writer described me as "the beatnik priest." Another member of the same fraternity dubbed me "the expresso priest"—expresso, not espresso, because of Expresso Nights I had organized, primarily as a means of individual and corporate expression.

At that time, I am sure some people in the small midwestern college town, where this fracas exploded, thought of coffee houses as settings for sex orgies, consumption of straight scotch in innocent looking coffee mugs, and "beatnik-communist" political meetings. It is almost amusing now to observe how coffee houses are "in," with a real sheen of respectability. Truisms aside, I guess time manages a lot of healing.

Coffee houses present an opportunity for meeting and discussion away from both stodgy Establishment halls and rules geared to perpetuating the status quo. For this very reason, we must make sharp demands on coffee houses. It is imperative that they not grow soft in fashion or fall easy prey to the decadence of celebrity. We must endeavor to cultivate—or not get in the way of—authentic community affirming itself in coffee houses. In all honesty, I must say that I have not yet found in any coffee house the quality of intense community which I have experienced on occasion in "Freedom Houses" in Mississippi and Alabama. Such a sense of community is an ideal to be nurtured in the burgeoning coffee houses.

John Perry has rightly begun this book with an examination of theology. He relates coffee houses to evangelism and the theology of the laity: Only having accomplished this, does he move from the "what" and "why" to the pragmatic "how." His treatment of the "how" is immensely useful. It is applicable—for example, when he talks about lay training of volunteers—to situations far removed from coffee house walls. So he has written a relevant book about coffee houses, but also managed to produce a highly practical handbook concerning the theology of the laity related to life in the world.

He encourages the church's mission in coffee houses, while cautioning against shallow caricatures of evangelism. It made me recall the movement of one campus coffee house into a church-related setting. Inside the new environment there was a supportive "in group" on hand to dull the tension of actual confrontation; props, a ready claque, and an agenda replaced the exciting, realistic possibilities of actual mission. The theology of mission must be related to this vast new network of coffee houses springing up to play an important part in our culture.

The church's theology has too often been fuzzy and, indeed, its life quite sick, when it has dichotomized between "holy" and "worldly." When this has occurred, an overt piosity has intruded itself; the arts have been held suspect, and even been perverted to serve a "religious" purpose; puritanism has been permitted to stifle the gospel's freedom. Church-related coffee houses must retain a radical spirit. They must bear marks of spontaneity, naturalness, and an unmistakable desire that all persons be integrated freely. All this needs to be accomplished without either paternalism or stiff pride in doing a "good work." John Perry's book has been sorely needed, and it points the way toward an honest Christian examination of an engrossing, highly significant movement within the modern church.

INTRODUCTION

In the early 1960's there was an epidemic of resignations from the pastoral ministry by young clergymen who refused to waste their time with triviality and traditional "churchy" activities. An increasing number of churchmen began to participate publicly in the dramatic struggle for civil rights in America. At the same time, a less dramatic epidemic—spawned by the same germ of discontent—was spreading quietly across the country. At first the participation of churchmen in coffee houses was a highly suspect activity. At that time—not without reason—coffee houses were thought to be among the worse forms of evil. Beatniks (i.e., people who wear beards!), not to mention prostitutes, dope peddlers, and subversives, were associated in the popular mind with these dimly lighted basement hangouts.

The coffee house epidemic first broke into the clear light of day in 1963, with the publication of *The Call to Commitment,* by Elizabeth O'Conner, associate on the staff of the hitherto unknown Church of The Savior in Washington, D. C. The wider church was astounded to learn that, far from being a devilish mistake, the coffee house ministry was the result of some very clear and profound—even radical—rethinking about the nature of the church and its ministry in the world. Within a year, the number of churches undertaking this new form of ministry doubled, from twenty to forty. Then it doubled again, so that there were about one hundred by January 1965. In the summer of 1965, the Coffee House Study Project discovered almost two hundred projects in forty-two states, Australia, Canada, and England; by spring of 1966, there were over

1,000 projects. The denominations, which had already begun to publish occasional news articles about coffee houses in their house organs, responded to this grass roots movement with materials describing the coffee house as a new and acceptable kind of missionary activity. The coffee house in now "in." What lies behind this rapid spread of the coffee house idea?

The coffee house ministry is the result of several divergent developments. Sociological criticism of the irrelevancies of traditional church activities and structures would have been useless without the radical rethinking about the theology of evangelism and the ministry of the laity which emerged in the circles and publications of the National and World Councils of churches in the late 1950's. The problem of communication in the modern world was already under investigation. We will explore these factors in the opening chapters.

The second part of the book is devoted to those mechanical details which are so important to those who are just getting started. The suggestions are intended to enlarge the perspective of those mapping out their own timetable of involvement. They will do little to alleviate the essential struggle of the ministry.

The concluding third of the book is intended to offer some ideas about organization and operation of the "living" coffee house itself. The chapters concern the interpersonal relationships of sponsors, managers, and volunteers, and the formal programming of coffee houses.

The material is organized with the conscious hope that the chapter divisions might well represent topics of discussion at successive weekly discussion meetings. The suggested readings which follow the early chapters are added in the hope—and conviction—that a few committees will get sufficiently aroused so that deeper investigations are warranted and profitable.

Part One: The Grounds of the Coffee House

WE ARE OPEN
SUN. NIGHTS
7:30 – 11 P.M.

WED.
AFT.'S
WOMEN'S
(ONLY)
COFFEE
CLATCH
2 PM.
to
4 PM

NEXT FRI.
AT 9: PM
MARTIN
MARTY
ASSOC. EDITOR OF
CHRISTIAN CENTURY

ANNOUNCING:
TWO 6WK. SEMINARS
#1 "MEANING of MATURITY"
Begins WED. NOV 3
8:00 461 W. MONTROSE
#2 "ETHICS + SOCIAL ACTION"
8:30 TUES. NOV. 9
St PAUL'S CHURCH

1. Evangelism

There are few activities of the Christian church in our generation which are more strategically important, more universally neglected, more commonly misunderstood, or more frequently prostituted than evangelism. It is historically one of the most central activities of the church's mission: and today it stands as a primary barrier to the ecumenical movement. Most ecumenics agree that divisions between the Protestant and Roman branches of Christendom are minor compared with the schism between "liberal" and "evangelical" Protestantism. It would be presumptuous to treat that whole problem in these pages, but we will focus on "evangelism," which is one of the central divisive issues.

Universally, evangelism is understood to be connected with the decision of faith and Christian conversion. It is that activity of the church, or churchmen, or Christians, which precedes the "decision." This is interpreted in two very different ways. Among the "evangelicals" and the "sects," the decision is an emotional, total response of the whole person to Jesus Christ, a commitment of one's life to him. In its most popular form, this view makes use of the "revival" and related techniques.

Among the "liberals" and the "churches" the decision is more rational than emotional, involves the conscious commitment of the person to the church of Jesus Christ, and takes expression more in membership enlistment than soul-saving. In our pluralistic society a given church may include members who lean each way, but these two options, which we will characterize as "revivalist" and "membershipist," account for almost everybody who is "for" evangelism.

The Common Error

But there are many who reject both of these options, and with them, the whole idea of evangelism. They believe that neither alternative, nor a combination, is appropriate—or at least, they do not feel called to engage with any enthusiasm in either the emotional conversion of souls or the rational enrollment of bodies. Evangelism is something which the other fellow does.

It is tempting for those who are trying to rethink the whole mission of the church to side with these anti-evangelists. Those who have taken potshots at Billygrahamism have described well the weaknesses of the emotional approach—superficiality, lack of educational follow-up, the incumbent biblical literalism, narrow theological viewpoint, and holier-than-thou mentalities. Unfortunately for those who would try to defend the revival, most of the criticisms are true.

It is also easy to reject the "join-the-church-of-your-choice" movement which has been with us since the late 1950's. We can hear the "noise of solemn assemblies" described in the recent sociological analyses of the Peter Bergers and Martin E. Martys. We have lived with an increase of "members" and concurrent decline in giving. We have seen that the church has sacrificed quality for quantity. We have been forced to admit that one hundred half-Christians is *not* necessarily better than fifty committed souls.

Unfortunately, those who would support one of the two options usually think that they are better off than their competitors. But a closer analysis of the situation reveals that the revivalists and the membershipists have more in common with each other than they would like to admit. To illuminate this common flaw, we must examine the ideas which lie behind "evangelism."

The primary material basis of evangelism is the "good news" of the New Testament. The phrase "good news" may refer to a singular event or activity of God, but it also was meant and used to encompass a large group of prophetic phrases going back to the Old Testament. We can agree that there is "one gospel," as Paul protested against the Corinthians' factions, but in our hindsight we can also acknowledge that there were and are many human ways of talking about the one gospel. We might look for an analogy in Paul S. Minear's book, which finds no less than ninety-six "images of the church in the New Testament." We could find dozens of metaphors and images for the "good news"—the Savior, Lord, Mighty Counselor, Redeemer, King, Emmanuel, High Priest, Prophet, Servant, Anointed One, Jesus, the Christ, Jesus Christ, and Christ Jesus. These are more than simply different "titles" of the one person—they belong to sometimes very different theological contexts.

Dr. Minear was not troubled by the diversity because, he concluded, the words were but frail human attempts to point to an overwhelming divine reality which both guaranteed and limited the images men used to discuss it. In the same way, we are forced by the pluralistic situation today to admit that there are many images for the "good news," and it is only a little bit helpful to know that your conversationalist may be high Anglican or low Baptist; such is the diversity of images.

But even when we can agree on the richness of the images of the "good news," what are we to do with it? "Preach the gospel" has become more a cliché today than it ever was in Paul's time. In fact, if we examine Scripture a little more carefully, we are forced to conclude that it is *not* really the all-inclusive divine injunction that some people like to believe. It is not too farfetched to blame this distorted interpretation of Scripture on the historical domination of our churches by "preachers." We will get back to the revival of interest in the laity in the next chapter, but for the time being let us remember that even more frequently the disciples were sent out to *preach, teach,* and *heal.* Paul acknowledges the division of labors and gifts, but we have in our day perhaps made the separation too clean. Preaching, teaching, and healing *are* separately definable, but *together* they make up the work of the church. The church cannot just "preach" and leave the teaching and healing to other people, times, and places.

So far we have two implications for the task of the church in its evangelical mission. We must allow the full richness of the diverse images of the good news in Scripture to be present in our own society, and we must bring some unity into the separate elements of our mission. These would seem to be contradictory implications, and, indeed, it is by achieving unity at the price of a rich diversity of theological images that the revivalism option thrives today, just as the membership option thrives on the opposite approach—it accepts diversity of images at the price of unity of purpose.

There is one fact which can save us from both these errors. We must remember, and incorporate into our planning, that the diverse images do indeed point to a single reality, the incarnate Lord (if we may single out one image to describe that reality). Moreover, that one reality, we have been told and confess to believe, is the "resurrected" Lord, who is "alive," continuing to carry out his work through the gift of his Holy Spirit—or, as the gospel writers all affirm, he goes with his disciples into the world.

Now the "resurrection" is a problematic concept for many Christians today. But the problem may in fact be that too often we think that the historical-empirical problem must be decided first—Did Jesus *really* rise up from the dead? This question may be an interesting option for cocktail parties or dormitory bull sessions, but the empirical issues are really quite secondary to the theological ones. Whatever "resurrection" may mean empirically is quite beside the point. Theologically, it means that the Christ is the one who is "out in the field" directing the church's mission from the front lines, as it were. It means that having the right jargon about the good news is secondary to being on the right battlefield. It means that it is not our battle but his.

Traditionally, this is expressed in a variety of images. We are spoken of as co-workers with Christ. (But this image is limited because it sometimes leads to thoughts of equality.) We are spoken of as witnesses to what he is doing. (But this image is also limited, since "witness" implies the judicial setting, a merely verbal explanation, eliminating the element of personal participation.) As a corrective, perhaps we need to stress more frequently the image of Christ working in us, as the power which motivates and the mind which guides our activities. This imagery preserves the distinctness of Christ without eliminating our own ethical responsibility for action. It allows us to discuss our actions in the light of his historical activities.

The "Signs"

The gospel writers frequently refer to "signs" of power in Jesus' healing and preaching work. The "signs" validate and vindicate the ministry of Jesus. In Mark 16:20, for example, we read that the disciples "went forth and preached everywhere, while the Lord worked with them *and confirmed the message by the signs that attended it."* (We must remember that "preached" in this context refers not simply to our kind of "sermon," but would have included, for instance, activities similar to those of Oral Roberts, the healing-preacher.)

What role do "signs" play in the contemporary church? The common flaw of both the revivalist and membershipist evangelists is that they *both* interpret the biblical idea of "signs" as being signs of *response from* the person evangelized. Billy Graham started out counting "souls saved" in response to his revivals as a sign of their validity. When he became more sophisticated, he switched to counting "inquirers"—but the idea is still the same; signs are understood as signs of *response from* the person who hears or sees. In a like manner, the membershipist evangelists interpret "signs" to be the *response of* individuals to the invitation to join this or that congregation. An increasing membership roster is thought to be a "sign" that the preaching is successful. A minister might confess "I must be doing something right." A recent cartoon showed a minister, seated in his study after the service, frantically rereading his sermon. Before him is an overflowing plate of offerings, and he is asking the deacon, "What *did* I say?"

The exact nature of this common error is seen more clearly when we examine the "signs" of, for instance, the pentecost story. There the flames which appear on the heads of the apostles *do not come from* the apostles (as signs that they got the Holy Spirit), but, and the text is very clear, they came *to* the apostles, *from* heaven. The signs are not of the apostles' human response to the Holy Spirit, but represent instead the power of the Holy Spirit himself coming to the church. In Mark, and elsewhere, the signs are not signs of response from the evangelized *or* recruited, but signs of power which accompany the message and mission of the church.

It is not easy to convince people, with their deeply rooted

ideas of success, that the powerful carrying out of the church's mission cannot be measured in terms of response. But it is essential to try. The "success" of the church consists not in men's response to her message, but in the faithfulness of her message—and all of her life—to the commission given her by her Lord. If she is faithfully following her Lord, her Lord will be out in front of her, providing the direction and power for the members of that body.

Matthew teaches us that "it is enough for the disciple to be like his master." Jesus did not compel those whom he confronted to accept him or his message. In our modern psychoanalytic way of thinking, we might say that he was self-confident about the validity of his message. At the same time he respected the freedom of the other to accept or reject him. The supreme illustration of this is in his confrontation with Pilate. Pilate asks him if all these claims about Jesus are true, and Jesus merely replies, in effect, "What do you think?" It is not, as we might preconclude, that Jesus "failed" here. Rather, Pilate simply exercised his God-given right to deny God. If we are to settle for being "like" our master, we will have to accept the same limitations. We can preach, teach, and heal in his name, but we cannot demand any particular response from those who hear. They must be free to love God freely, or not at all. Nor can we gauge our faithfulness by men's response to our living messages. It is perfectly true that a good tree will always bear good fruit—but we cannot force men to take and eat that good fruit, any more than Jesus forced Pilate to love him.

Our exegesis of the Marcan passage has not yet exhausted itself. If the signs that accompany the message of the disciples confirmed it, is it asking too much to suggest that we apply the same criterion to our own messages? What are the "signs" which accompany the Word the world hears from us? What are (in modern idiom) the nonverbal components of our message and its proclamation? We preach, for instance, that Jesus befriended publicans and sinners. But we usually do it in a context which makes it unlikely that we will be called upon to befriend the same groups! As Dietrich Bonhoeffer says in *Life Together,* most of our congregations would be unthinkably horrified if a *real* sinner were discovered in their midst. But this seldom happens, since sinners in our generation see many signs which warn them to stay away from religious buildings. Jesus may have befriended publicans and sinners, but we have made it quite plain that only the righteous may inherit the women's parlor.

What are the "signs" that accompany our message in these circumstances? It is quite clear to the world that religion is for the righteous. The signs say that "Jesus came to save the righteous," contradicting, rather than supporting, our message. It does not take too much imagination to think of other messages which are accompanied by contrary signs.

But what signs would accompany our message and give confirming support to it? We say, in part, "God loves this world which he created" What signs accompanying this message would give powerful confirmation to it? Signs of care, signs of love, indications of concern! The Lord working in and through and alongside his disciples, confirming their words. The coffee house building is itself a concrete (!) sign of concern for the nameless faces of the metropolis and the lonely masses of students on campus.

Another proclamation is "Christ died to set you free." If there is any compulsiveness in the proclaimers, the accompanying signs clearly contradict the message. The only sign which would "confirm" that message is the presence of genuine personal freedom in the lives of the coffee house workers themselves.

If we are to preach that Jesus came to save sinners, we must do it in a context that permits people to really *be* sinners, and *then* be "saved." Piety cannot be a precondition for salvation, nor for our fellowship. The contrast between the coffee house and the traditional church supper is strongest at this point. Only the righteous are served at the supper, but all manner of sinners find their way into the coffee house. This situation is distressing to those who have forgotten that they too are sinners, essentially no different from the coffee house customers.

We spoke earlier of the need to bring the full richness of diverse imagery into our evangelistic effort. We spoke also of the need to unify our various ministries into an approach to the "whole person." Now we have added the dimension of bringing power to our ministry, the power of confirming signs. But "signs" have a double-

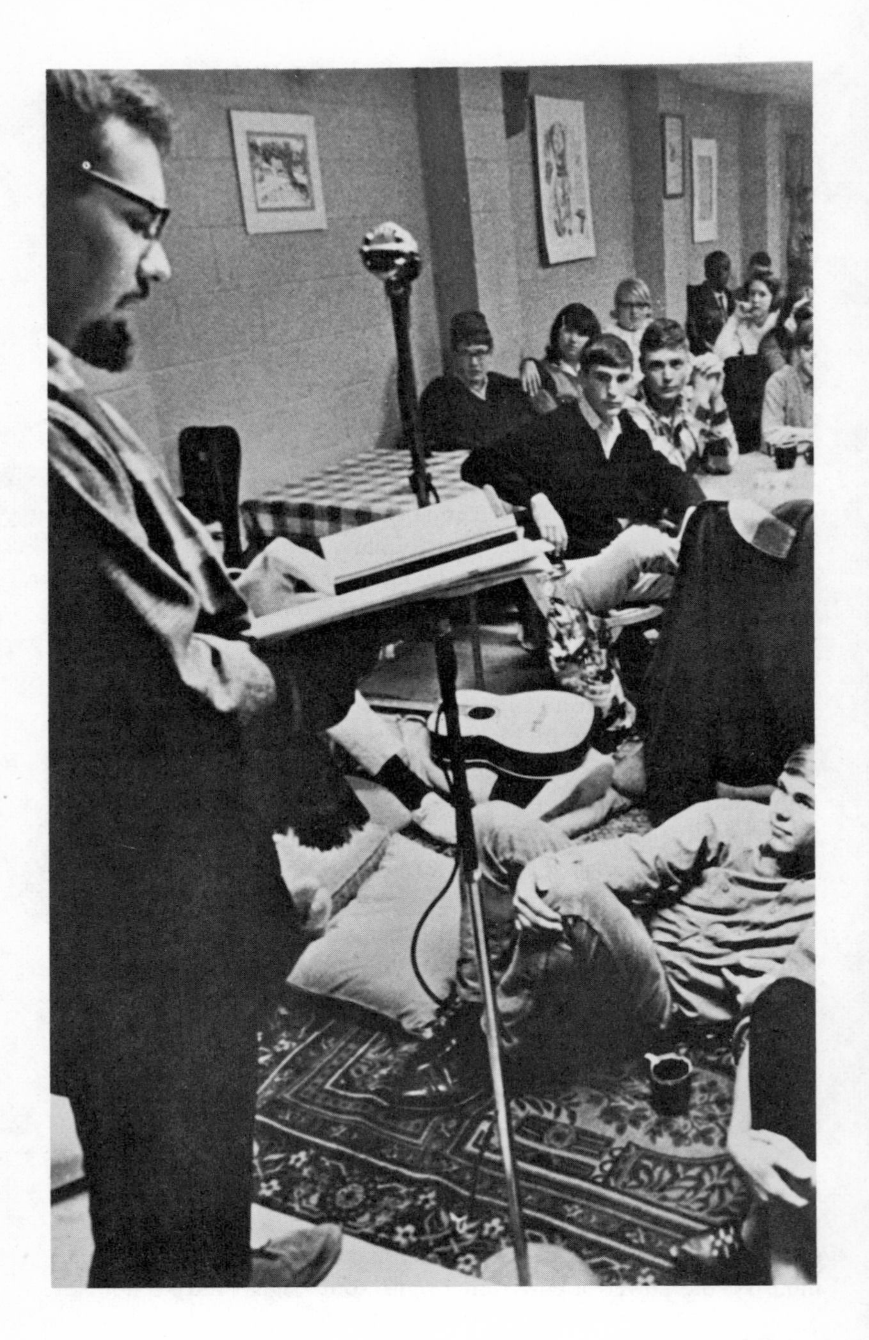

edged meaning. They point forward to the observer, impressing his consciousness; but they also point backward to the source of that power. If the only source of "power" is the human weakness of those who participate in the coffee house ministry, the signs will not be any stronger than that. But if the coffee house ministry (or any ministry) is itself a part of the ongoing ministry of the church of the Lord Jesus Christ and participates in his strength as it proclaims his gospel, then it will be a powerful ministry and a faithful evangelism. If there is any "response" to the message, it will be because men in their freedom have chosen to accept it, and him. All we can do is be faithful disciples. That is all we have been asked to do.

FOR FURTHER STUDY . . .

Concept. World Council of Churches, Department of Studies in Evangelism. Issued quarterly.

A Monthly Newsletter About Evangelism. World Council of Churches, Division of World Mission and Evangelism.

Lesslie Newbigin. *Trinitarian Faith and Today's Mission*. John Knox Press, 1964.

Theodore Otto Wedel. "Evangelism's Three-fold Witness: Kerygma, Liononia, Diakonia." *The Ecumenical Review*, Vol. IX, No. 3, April 1957. Reprinted separately.

A Theological Reflection on the Work of Evangelism. World Council of Church, special issue of the Division of Studies Bulletin, Vol. V, Nos. 1 and 2.

Colin Williams. *Where in the World?* and *What in the World?* National Council of Churches of Christ in the U.S.A., Office of Publication and Distribution.

2. The Theology of the Laity

The average layman will react with horror when we open the subject of the "ministry of the laity" . . . and rightly so. To most of us, the ministry of the laity involves our participation in "ministerial" functions, and we envision lay-led worship services, laymen making hospital calls, visiting the elderly, and, in short, relieving the minister of some of his traditional "duties." Some of us even suspect that the whole enterprise is a mistake. All of us find it a threat, a job for which we are unprepared and untrained.

It is. And this description, while admittedly a caricature, is nevertheless a caricature of a very real problem which plagues the church today. We have the mistaken notion that an increase in "ministry" on the part of the laity involves their increased participation in the "activities of the church." Nothing could be further from the truth.

The Recovery of the Laity

In a very real sense the problem goes back to the Council of Nicaea in A.D. 325, where the delineation of the true church around the decrees of the bishops was, thanks to imperial power, established as doctrinal fact. From that time on, the church has always looked to its clerical leadership for definition and direction. Of course there was nothing inherently wrong with this, but human nature being what it is, it was perhaps inevitable that the clergy should take *their* work as the model for the work of the *whole* church. Throughout history we have developed an image of the priest at the center of the life of the congregation, with helpers around him to aid and assist him in the performance of his duties.

On the face of it, there is nothing wrong with this, except for the entirely unjustified and unwarranted *assumption* that the clergy's job was the model for everyone's job. Even today we assume that this is the case. Whenever one of our members feels called of God, it is invariably in the direction of performing "ministerial" functions—one teaches Sunday school, leads worship services, starts a Bible study class. The way to become a "better" layman in our understanding is to become a "part-time" minister, or, still better, to give up one's job and enter "full-time Christian service." We operate on the assumption that the minister's job is the model of what all Christians should do "if they have the time."

A flood of literature in the past several years has begun to challenge this common viewpoint and its assumption, and with good reasons. The turning point was the publication, in 1959, of Hendrick Kraemer's *A Theology of the Laity.* This scholarly book explores in detail the traditional place of the layman in the church, the growing influence and finally domination of the clergy, and the present plight of the churches. Then Kraemer reaches back to pick up and stress some biblical and theological ideas which have been traditionally neglected, and puts them in a new light. For instance, he takes the relatively obvious biblical truth that God is concerned about the world which he created, and that he sent his Son into the world, on behalf of the world. The church, he concludes, participating in its Lord's ministry, exists on behalf of the world. Just as Jesus was sent into the world, the church is sent into the world; i.e., it has a *mission.* Jesus is the Anointed King, the hero of God's whole creation, but the manner in which he manifests himself is that of the suffering servant.

We speak of Jesus' *ministry,* translating the Greek word *diakonia,* which originally meant to serve, as in waiting on tables. When we speak of serving in the coffee house ministry, then, we are simply applying the original meaning of the biblical word for *serving.* In our present corrupt understanding, we have translated *diakonia* as *deacon,* one who helps serve the Christian ceremonial elements, but the original meaning is much wider than the designation of a ceremonial office. It meant service in the sense of a servant—a very humble job, indeed. Thus Kraemer concludes that *mission* and *ministry* were the two central facts which described the life of the earliest church. In other words, Jesus sent the church out into the world to minister unto it, just as he did. He defined the church, not in static terms, but in terms of the job that it was called to perform in the world.

Without suggesting for a moment that we spurn the contributions of those Christians who preceded us, in setting up the organization which we have inherited, the new literature seeks to *add* the concepts of the mission and ministry of the whole church to our understanding. The commissioning of the Lord for ministry is, in the Bible, a task which is laid upon *all* followers. Mission and ministry apply to the whole church.

Historically, the clergy emerged within the whole people of God as a specialized group whose task it was to prepare the rest for their work in the world. Kraemer argues that "the main part of the ministry of the clergy should be to enable the laity to fulfill their peculiar inalienable ministry" in the world. It is the job of the minister (clergyman) to train and prepare laymen for their work. This is quite the reverse of the presently accepted view, that it is the job of the laymen to help the minister perform his functions in the church! Kraemer argues that this viewpoint would signal a "radical reformation" in the church. He is quite right.

It must be confessed that the contributions of Kraemer and his kind are not entirely new. From time to time these ideas have come up before. We are quite accustomed, for instance, to think that every Christian has a "vocation" to exercise on the job. We are fond of quoting Martin Luther's idea of "the priesthood of all believers." But we often fail to remember that when Luther spoke of every man's calling to be a priest in and on the job, he was thinking of an era when men worked fourteen hours a day. Rather than just "on the job," Luther meant *all day long*—they were the same in his time, but we think differently because we work a forty-hour week. We now have many hours of leisure time available. It is tempting to think that some of this time might be spent in the internal work of the church, but it should not. If we are to take the theology of the laity seriously, we can perform our ministry as much in our recreation as Luther thought we could in our vocation. The ministry of the laity does not mean going into the church to help the minister on Wednesday afternoon. It means being a minister wherever one happens to be on Wednesday afternoon.

The Corporate Priesthood of All Believers

Protestants usually think that they have a special advantage over their Roman Catholic brethren, in the contributions which Luther and the reformers made to our understanding of the priesthood of all believers. Unfortunately, this is only partly true, because we also have a special disadvantage, in the form of our exaggerated idea of "individualism." Historically, the same stress on individualism that *freed* Protestants to engage in the priesthood of all believers also left them powerless to carry it out.

Without exception, our Protestant understanding of the ministry of the laity—up until recently—has been that the ministry is something which each individual does on his own after he leaves the inspiration of the sanctuary. We live with a dichotomization between the corporate activities of the church—worship, study, fellowship—and the individual activities of churchmen—witnessing in the world and ministering to our neighbors. Individuals are expected to become involved in the life of the secular community, to join the PTA and the Civil Rights Council, the service clubs and the town government—always as individuals.

The result of this individualized approach to the ministry of the laity is that when the individual gets out into the world and tries to "minister" he is completely unprepared and unable to do so. Either he feels so completely at sea, convinced that he is the only person on the school board or standing at the bar who has a spark of Christian love to share, that he keeps his mouth shut—or he becomes frightened and insecure and blabs platitudinous clichés about morality and Christianity and principles upon which our country was supposedly founded. Do not imagine that these illustrations are exaggerated either. We have many times observed situations in which we had hoped that someone would step forth with a theological viewpoint to enlighten and unburden the conversation. Just as often, we have been embarrassed when one of our brethren offered a stylized, oversimplified "Christian" answer to a complex problem. ("There ought to be a law against all the smut that they are selling on the newsstands these days. It's downright un-Christian!")

The results of silence are perfectly obvious. Nothing is accomplished, except that untold numbers of persons who have not heard the "good news" continue to live without it. The results of the blabbering "Christian" approach are less obvious and more devastating for the ministry. When easy answers are presented, nothing is accomplished. But more importantly, the world gains the clear impression that the church has nothing new to say. Hugh Hefner, for instance, represents a widely held opinion that what is needed in the area of sex is the elimination of vestiges of "the Christian idea" of sex. Those of us who struggle with sex ethics know that there is no such animal, but we can readily understand how the world has come to think we do advocate a single, simple answer.

We will turn in the next chapter to some considerations of the problem of communicating the good news in "dialogue" with the world. We are concerned here to point out that the major cause of our inept approach at the present time is that we are simply unprepared for any approach at all. We send our members out into the world, one by one. They become frightened by the enormity of the task, and respond in either one or the other extreme way, equally ineffective. Is there any solution to this problem?

We may draw a clue from the fact that Jesus sent his disciples out "two by two." Not even the most famous individualist of the apostles, Paul, was really alone on any of his trips, although our heroistic reading of the story often overlooks his constant companions. We are accustomed to singling out the "hero" of the biblical stories, forgetting that they always ministered in groups. It is at once a radical and a reassuring suggestion that present-day disciples could do no better than follow this example. The idea we present here has already been proved in many new situations. We need to develop corporate ministries of the laity.

A corporate ministry of the laity is one in which laymen work together, with the help of their clergy, at *their* ministry *in the world.* In the vocational sphere, this is already being done in many experimental "vocational" discussion and mission groups. In or near their place of work, groups of secretaries, of dentists, of doctors, and of salesmen sit down with their peers to discuss the common problems of ministering in their vocation. In the recreational sphere (which continues to claim a higher percentage of time) only a few projects are underway. These include, among others, the skiers ministry, and the "Christian Ministry in National Parks" program of the National Council of Churches. The coffee house ministry is just one of the new ministries which share this common new concern. The dynamics are distinctively different from traditional activities.

In most church-sponsored study groups, the pattern is usually unconsciously arrived at. A Bible study group, for instance, plods along from one chapter to the next, imitating the pastor's New Testament course in seminary. The unexamined goal of this procedure is to prepare laymen to be scholarly biblical exegetes—a talent essential for the clerical ministry, but unnecessary for the layman's ministry in the world. Once again we see that the clergy's job has become the model for the layman's work, instead of the other way around.

If we start instead with the assumption that laymen have a ministry to perform in the world, and that it is the clergy's job to help prepare them for *that* ministry, the shape of the Bible study would be very different indeed. The focus of the study would and should be the problems laymen have in communicating the good news which they hear in church and read in their Scriptures. Examples of real life situations are not simply "illustrations" of biblical truths; they are the arena into which our laymen must bring the good news.

The shift in focal point from training miniature ministers to preparing laymen for their own ministry in the world brings with it implications for the leadership of such groups. It should be perfectly obvious that the person least qualified to direct the ministry in the world is the minister. It is only because of the lack of qualified lay leadership that clergymen are justified in taking initiative in organizing various lay ministry groups. We can hope that their leadership will be gradually transferred to laymen, so that the clergy themselves will be freed to perform their own ministries better.

The ministry of the clergy is to equip and train the saints for their ministry in the world. To this end the clergy are and need be prepared as the theological specialists who take the time to secure an overall theological education, that they will have the appropriate skills and knowledge for the laymen to call upon.

The Ministry of the Laity in the Coffee House

The coffee house movement provides an excellent experimental situation for the whole church to explore the implications of the new theology of the laity. If we try to apply our previous misconceptions to the ministry in the coffee house, we would for instance have clergymen serve as waiters, for laymen customers. (This is modeled on the clerically dominated ritual of communion.) A few coffee houses actually make this mistake. In the absence of sufficient numbers of clergy, the ones available serve as "bartenders." In operation this pattern meets some of the goals of the coffee house movement, but it completely sidesteps the issue of the laity.

Another misconception applied would allow laymen to serve as waiters, without any special training for their service. This is our common view of individual witness moved indoors. The mistake comes in thinking that every person is naturally endowed to be a minister, without any special training for his ministry.

Still another misconception which sometimes turns up is the idea that anyone in off the street is able to serve as a waiter. This position makes the mistake of thinking the world has already assimilated the distinctively Christian idea of the suffering servant. It hasn't, as the rapid turnover of staffs under this arrangement proves.

If we incorporate our new understanding of the theology of the laity, and the subordinate theology of the clergy, the pattern which emerges involves laymen serving as waiters and workers in the coffee house. The same laymen meet, from time to time, with their theological specialist and pastoral counselor, the clergyman, for special training for their job. The laymen learn to minister to the customers, and to each other. The clergyman, insofar as he is by definition also a layman, participates in the coffee house just as

anyone else. Insofar as he is a clergyman, set apart for a specific job, he functions to help the others do their job better.

We will discuss specific elements of the training program in Chapter Eight. Before the practical details, we turn our attention to the relationship between laymen and customers.

FOR FURTHER STUDY . . .

Francis Ayers. *The Ministry of the Laity.* Westminster, 1962.

Yves Congar. *Lay People in the Church.* Rev. by M. J. Congar. Newman, 1965.

Howard Grimes. *The Rebirth of the Laity.* Abingdon, 1962.

Hendrick Kraemer. *A Theology of the Laity.* Westminster, 1959.

Stephen Neill and Hans-Ruedi Weber. *The Layman in Christian History.* Westminster, 1963.

Hans-Ruedi Weber. *Salty Christians.* Seabury, 1963.

Laity. Nos. 2-6. World Council of Churches, Department of the Laity, May 1962. Special reprint.

FOLK MUSIC
TONIGHT

3. Dialogue and Donuts

In the previous chapter we cautioned against thinking of "signs of response" as vindications of one's proclamation and mission. But we were not suggesting that the church should continue its present policy of preaching without listening for feedback. There is a significant difference between looking for "success" and assessing the successfulness of our proclamation. By successfulness of our proclamation we refer not to the spiritual responses which people make, but to the effectiveness of our speaking and the accuracy of their hearing. That is, we are not asking whether Pilate accepted Jesus—we are asking whether Pilate understood what it was he was rejecting. The ironies of the Gospel of John make it plain that Pilate heard Jesus, but only with his external ears—he "heard but did not hear," in the prophet's sense.

Our concern is whether the world hears our proclamation even with the external ears. John Vannersdale, in preparing materials for "The Unmuzzled Ox" at Cornell, wrote: "If one listens seriously to large segments of the campus population, it soon becomes clear what these students have *already* heard from the church is not the gospel."

This problem is prior to the question of men's response to the gospel. It asks whether men have, in fact, even heard the gospel at all, and the usual honest answer is that they have not. Pilate's speeches in W. H. Auden's *For The Time Being* present an unusually sensitive treatment of a man wrestling with the implications of the "good news." But the speeches which the church hears in the open conversation of the coffee house more often reveal people struggling with moralism, provincialism, legalism, and religious sentimentality. They have heard the religious words, but they have not been confronted by the gospel. Indeed, we have already gotten some feedback from our listening post in the coffee house.

Most Americans see the church as preaching moralism and absolutism. The religious sequence is that through righteous living one becomes a Christian. (Paul's sequence, in contrast, was you are saved, therefore *be* righteous in living.) This view is held as much by those who have separated from the church as by those who retain their affiliation.

It is easy for us to see the error involved, but it is not easy for us to convince those in error that they miss the point of the good news. They have been convinced, by their own experience, that there are no real sinners permitted in the congregation of the righteous. They know that no one in our churches admits to being a sinner, save perhaps in a liturgical sense. Pietism has long dominated the American religious establishment.

Franklin Littell's masterpiece *From State Church to Pluralism* describes without the usual romanticism the rapid growth of our American population, and the sheer inability of the churches to expand fast enough, to educate their members. So many Americans have only a superficial acquaintance with Christian thought. This "too many too soon" problem, together with the habitually pietistic stance, has left the church in a world which misunderstands what little it has heard, and has not even heard the whole story.

Put this misunderstanding into the context of vocational specialization, and the problem becomes even more complex. Not only do we have misunderstanding, but we have such an overwhelming "communication" problem that it is doubly difficult for the church to proclaim its message and be understood.

Another dimension to the communications problem is related to pluralism. There is such a cross-fertilization of denominational backgrounds in most of our churches that the all-important subtleties of theological language are often misunderstood, even by the devout of all faiths. In the ecumenical context of most of our campus ministry, even the clergy of differing traditions have trouble understanding each other. How much more difficult are the problems of laymen, who are usually educated only in their own religious tradition.

The solution to the present dilemma is, of course, dialogue. This concept of communication has been so much talked and written about that there is no need to go into detail. We would refer the reader to the church library, where a copy of Reuel Howe's *The Miracle of Dialogue* is sure to be found. This rich study book has already been used in many coffee house training groups. In addition, the field of small group dynamics, both in the church and in sociology and psychology, is rich with theoretical books and handbooks. The only thing which the coffee house is able to add to this field is the opportunity to practice the art of dialogue. A certain paragraph has made its way onto the back page of more than one coffee house menu: "This is an age which has produced volumes on the need for real communication, while providing little opportunity for the experiencing of it."

We must confess that it is a bit of an anachronism to find "dialogue" discussed in the same old-fashioned Women's Sewing Circles and Reading Clubs; but this is usually what happens. It is a little like reading travel books without taking a vacation! Is there any wonder that "dialogue" has become a cliché without ever having been tried? The coffee house provides an opportunity to experience dialogue, not just to talk about it. It is a missionary structure of the congregation in which the form is shaped by the interpersonal relationships sought there.

New Structures for Ministry

Those who are accustomed to the traditional churchy activities will find several new features in the coffee house. It differs sharply from the church supper, which draws only those who are willing to play the social niceties game: to smile all evening, to engage no one in threatening conversation, and to reveal nothing personal or intimate which would embarrass the other party. Admittedly, this game is relatively easy to play, because one may be assured that only the "right kind" of people will be present. But the church supper serves only the church.

When the church opens its doors to serve the whole world, all sorts and conditions of men may accept the offer to dine at our Table. Some have no sympathy, or even respect, for our cherished traditions. Imagine waiting on someone who didn't think Christianity had all the answers! It is one thing to see such people walking the streets of every town, and quite another to serve them coffee. It is one thing to know there are such persons, and quite another to meet them socially.

Yet we know, in our hearts, that Jesus spent only a few short hours of his ministry in the upper room, and we have heard and believed that God sent his Son because he loved the world. It is so easy to talk about these things in the Sunday school classroom, and so difficult to change our traditional churchy patterns of activity. But there must be a change, if we are to benefit from these new theological understandings, and the change must be really radical. Indeed, the radicalness which we are advocating is no less than the difference between the in-group church supper and the open-door coffee house.

If the coffee house is itself a radically new setting for the church, so is the kind of activity that takes place there. We will discuss specific kinds of programs in a later chapter, but here we are concerned with the patterns of relationships between the church and the world in the coffee house. If the reader will permit a slight caricature, there are two general patterns now in practice. In "evangelistic" activities the church takes the lead by "presenting" its point of view, urging acceptance of it, and answering questions about it. In "service" type activities, the church quietly sneaks into the world—the town fair, the school board, the Community Chest Council—and keeps its mouth shut. There is no middle ground. It is (properly) considered inappropriate to discuss theology on the YMCA basketball court.

The genius of the coffee house is that it cuts across the traditional categories of evangelism and service. It can be seen as a "service project," but here the "service" *includes* talking about what is important in one's life. For those who are believers, this will quite naturally include talking about one's faith. Since conversation is one of the main *raison d'être*'s of the coffee house, we do not suspect the overly interested waitress to be soliciting for some illegal vice. Warm and friendly human conversation is to be expected, and accepted. Indeed, we must even expect discussion of intimate or serious subjects.

The distinctive characteristics of the coffee house location combine to facilitate the kind of conversation we call "dialogue." The most obvious contribution lies in the worldly appearance of the coffee house. No one viewpoint's distinctive symbols decorate the walls and lend their silent support to the arguments of either side. Seated before a minister in the pulpit, one cannot help but anticipate certain ideas, depending on whether the central symbol is a cross, the open Bible, or a display of flowers. But no one's mind can be predisposed by the "ordinary" appearance of the coffee house. (On the other hand, the Christian volunteers cannot count on religious decorations to support the truth of their beliefs either!) The result is that the coffee house is, in appearance, religiously neutral.

It is this neutrality which makes it a safe place for both volunteer and customer. Neither need feel compromised by drinking coffee here. Church membership recruiters assume that half the battle is won by getting people into the church building. In a sense, they are right, since one must acquiesce to a degree to merely enter the holy places. But a skeptic, agnostic, or critic can participate in the coffee house without first giving in or up. This same neutrality provides freedom for the Christian volunteers, also. No one is forced, even by mental habit, to "act religious" in the coffee house. No one is forced by the surroundings to "defend God."

The neutrality of the coffee house is a powerful weapon. Used honestly, it can be a powerful sign that Christians do not need to pull any punches. It goes without saying, however, that this same power can be used for evil. Let us hope that the coffee house is not used merely as a "front," to draw unsuspecting sinners in off the streets and convert them (unwittingly) to our point of view. Regrettably, this is the conscious purpose of some coffee houses presently in operation.

In the coffee house ministry the good news cannot, unfortunately, be presented in any ordinary manner. Simply to move into the coffee house the liturgical and conversational forms which have been developed in the sanctuary would show the grossest misunderstanding of both the liturgy and the coffee house. It would betray a lack of seriousness in the reformation of the church. The major task confronting the coffee house ministry today is the development of appropriate vocabularies and modes of discussion, for that pluralistic theological context. The chief heuristic value of the coffee house ministry may well be that it serve as a testing ground for the churches' dialogue with the post-Christian world. Answers that come too easy, too early, will only disappoint us and drive us back to the traditional activities.

In the geographical locations where coffee house ministries are usually born, it is not necessary to duplicate the traditional activities of the church in the coffee house program. Everyone has theoretical access to worship services, Sunday school classes, youth groups, and the like. We must be willing to admit that the main reason people don't come is that they don't *want* to come. It would be an insult to their freedom simply to offer more of the same in a new setting. Instead, we must strive to develop new alternative ways of presenting the good news.

The first step in the process requires the church to *listen* in the coffee house to what the world is saying. She must listen to hear what the world has already heard from the church. She must listen to hear what the world understands by the things it has heard. She must listen to hear what the world thinks it needs. She must listen to hear what the world thinks it is being offered by the church. Then—quietly—the church can retreat to her upper rooms, confess her sins, reflect upon her observations, and begin to develop new kinds of presentations of the good news for the future.

If the church sincerely follows through in her attempt to listen to the world, she will discover that her message has sometimes been heard, internalized, and so translated that it becomes difficult, but not impossible, for the church to recognize it. The declaration on Religious Liberty of Vatican Council II is an excellent illustration of this process. The Council Fathers recognized that modern ideas of the "dignity of the person," far from being a contradiction of Christian principles, are in fact a manifestation of the "leaven of the gospel" going about "in quiet work in the minds of men."

Enthusiasts are often fond of describing loyalty to Jesus Christ like pregnancy—either you are or you aren't. That may be quite true, insofar as men are concerned. But the language by which they communicate is neither Christian nor pagan—it is itself neutral, and used by all kinds of men. Too often we judge agreement between persons by the similarity of their vocabulary systems; and, conversely, we estimate a greater divergency than may in fact be present in language differences. One of the firstfruits of "listening" in the coffee house has been the discovery that the apparent differences between men are often not the real ones.

It is no accident that a variety of art forms have emerged in the coffee house ministry to convey meaning and content. We have already examined some of the reasons why mere words are ineffective in promoting communication in our pluralistic context. Words are also biased in appealing primarily to the intellectual side of man. If our ministry is to be a unified approach to the "whole person," we need forms which convey emotion as well as reason. This is one more reason for the essentially artistic mode of communication in coffee house programming. The majority of coffee houses permit, in their formal programming, only artistic modes of communication—folk singing, poetry, and painting are most common. Even those who permit more rational forms of communication mix them sparingly with the artistic forms.

The theoretical goal of all coffee house programming is to raise questions, rather than give answers. We have grown accustomed to the rhetorical questions that open so many sermons. Will anyone believe that we do not have a ready answer up our collective sleeve? The essential informality of the coffee house operates to convince all that the questioning is sincere. Psychologically, formality of structure invites rigidity of thought, while informality breeds flexibility and open-mindedness. Since these characteristics are essential to dialogical communication, the coffee house must of necessity be informal in structure.

After a public lecture, the coffee hour is an informal break which permits and encourages conversation and discussion. The presence of food in an informal setting distinguishes the coffee break from the "question and answer period," which is employed when the lecturer only wishes to clarify his argument. A question and answer period is not, by this definition, what we seek in the coffee house ministry. The food—however simple—is an essential factor in the informality, and thus the openness of coffee house conversation. Donuts will not guarantee dialogue, but they will facilitate it.

Some critics of the coffee house movement are quick to point out that beer would lubricate the dialogical mechanism even more readily than coffee. And, they are perfectly right. But the church is not ready for beer. Our only consolation is that the Apostle Paul thought the young Corinthian Christians were only able to digest milk; we have at least graduated to a stronger brew. Perhaps the descendants of the coffee house ministry will be sent into bars and taverns.

FOR FURTHER STUDY . . .

Reuel Howe. *The Miracle of Dialogue*. Seabury, 1963.

"Small Groups in the Church." *Pastoral Psychology,* June 1964.

Sara Little. *Learning Together in the Christian Fellowship*. John Knox Press, 1956.

Dietrich Bonhoeffer. *Life Together*. Harper, 1954.

John Casteel. *Spiritual Renewal Through Personal Groups*. Association, 1957.

"Renewal in the Churches." *Union Seminary Quarterly Review,* Vol. XVI, No. 3, March 1961.

Heije Faber and Ebel van der Schoot. *The Art of Pastoral Conversation*. Abingdon, 1965.

Part Two: Cups and Saucers

DOOR
THE
DOOR

4. Locations and Decorations

Purpose of the Coffee House

The first step in planning for a coffee house is to formulate a statement of purpose. A statement may be only the norm from which all things deviate, but it is important to have a statement by which to judge the subordinate questions of decor, organization, etc. The mere existence of a statement is no indication of the extent to which it will be internalized by the volunteers, however; nor is it any guarantee that the intentions will in fact be carried through. But it does provide a reference point for the committee in those rare and valuable moments of self-criticism and honest reflection.

Many coffee house committees have been concerned about the degree of theological explicitness which "should" be manifest in a statement of purpose. Such concern reflects a mistaken view of the uses to which such statements are actually put. If the statement has theological integrity, there is nothing to be feared by making it very explicit. If the statement is subversive of the integrity of the potential customers, no amount of subtlety will disguise the fact. We Christians need to remind ourselves that the objections of the atheist are not primarily repudiations of our thought, but of our lives; our agnostic friends would like to believe that we can defend with our lives what we proclaim with our lips.

A number of factors need to be taken into account in the statement of purpose: there should be certain affirmations about the nature of the world, of those who serve, and of those who are served. And, if these two groups emerge strikingly different, the statement should probably go back to committee. Malcolm Boyd, in an essay, "And the Church Decided to Open a Coffee House . . . A Fable," satirizes the holier-than-thou approach: "We want dialogue with YOU . . . we seek with YOU an I-Thou encounter . . . We want to love YOU and be loved by YOU . . ."

A theologically accurate statement of purpose will have to take into account the empirical similarities between Christians and nonbelievers, while presenting the eschatological differences in meaningful ways. That is to remind us that Christians are only "different" in their faith and in service to Christ; they remain sinners in and of themselves.

Some two hundred church-related coffee houses, with about 175 different names, have come to our attention. Only a handful are repeats, "The Fish" (or its Greek equivalent, "Ichthus") being the most common. Most coffee house committees seem to sweat out a name which has symbolic significance *in the local setting.* The selection of a name takes into account the needs—and prejudices—of both the workers and the customers. As a kind of shorthand statement of the purpose, the "name" serves a useful pedagogical device, incarnating in symbolism the mission of the coffee house. Not all names are drawn from biblical symbolism, however. Many have secular significance—"The Celler," the "Back Door," "The Exit."

A name sometimes helps to provide a motif for decoration of the coffee house. "The Sign of the Tarot" has large tarot cards on the walls. "The Fishnet" has a Cape Cod decor, with candles in corks on the tables and fishnets hanging from the ceiling. Other kinds of names do not imply any particular decor, but suggest program emphasis, or the ultimate purpose of the coffee house. But the most important value of the name is the impression it creates in potential customers, for the name is usually the first thing which they hear about the coffee house. If it sounds like a place where they will be at ease, they may try to find out.

Purpose and Decor: Integrity

The location and decoration of the coffee house should be a manifestation of its purpose. One would hardly expect that a coffee house designed to serve, for instance, the beatnik population, would be a side room opening off the church vestibule. One cannot serve the inner city from the suburbs; a campus coffee house cannot simply lure students downtown to the great stone cathedral. On the other hand, if one of the purposes of the coffee house is to engage the church with the world, one must find a location where both the church and the world feel at home.

It is perfectly obvious that most church buildings, and most of their rooms, are not suitable places for such encounters, without alterations. Church rooms are among the most stylized decorations in the whole creation, with bronze plaques, stiff chairs, sanitary tile, and a number of other identifying characteristics. So one cannot honestly expect the non-church member to be at home in such buildings.

Under the circumstances, there are two options, with vastly different consequences involved in each. Either some existing church-owned room must be renovated, or some non-church properties leased. A good deal of money is involved in the later option, so that sides are pretty well drawn among existing coffee houses about which option is "best." Actually, both options have advantages and disadvantages.

The advantages of the non-church properties are manifold: it is traditional for a coffee house to be located in a commercial store-front district. It is usually more accessible for the clientele. It provides a better image of the "church-in-the-world," a kind of "market-place" Christianity which is vogue (and rightly so!). Finally, the removal of the coffee house from one church's building opens the door to multiple sponsorship and, therefore, a more ambitious budget.

But the more ambitious budget is in part necessary, because the biggest disadvantage of the store-front is cost. Not only are the choicest locations expensive to rent—they frequently require extensive renovation and interior decoration. Coffee houses have been put in former supermarkets, laundromats, art print stores, and taverns. In addition, the store-front coffee house must be entirely self-contained. Rest rooms, kitchen facilities, storage facilities, and other basic needs must be provided. But the biggest disadvantage appears only in strategic, long-term thinking. With the coffee house physically removed from the church, it is *easier* for it to become theoretically isolated. If the coffee house suffers too greatly from this isolation from the source of its inspiration, it will die. But what is more likely is that the good things which are learned there about the church-in-the-world will never get fed back into the life and ministry of the whole church which initiated the coffee house. It will become a kind of quasi-acceptable mission station for those who cannot "fit in" the traditional ongoing life of the congregation. The Ladies' Aid and the Christian Endeavor programs will go on, as they always have, without ever coming to grips with the lessons learned in the coffee house.

Those avant-garde souls who are planning Elmtown's first church-sponsored coffee house will no doubt think that their biggest hurdle is getting their plans through the conservative Board of Trustees. That may pose a temporary problem, but most disciples who have passed that test now agree that the real problem is getting the church boards to take *seriously* what is happening in the coffee house. The usual reaction is one of complete indifference, provided that no beer cans are found on the premises by the ever-snooping janitor, and no moral scandals evolve which might implicate the good people of the friendly church on the corner. They will otherwise pay little attention to this "fad." In extreme cases, the assistant minister will be let go a few months later, not for his coffee house, but for neglecting his traditional duties.

The two biggest disadvantages of the store-front are the two biggest advantages of the option to use church properties. There is no rental fee among the church organizations, and, while feedback is by no means guaranteed, the opportunities for it are greatly expanded. In cases where the man who does the preaching has an understanding of, if not a participation in, the coffee house, the feedback will be facilitated.

The availability of accessory rooms is an aspect of the cost which is not to be underestimated. Coffee houses located in church basements often have access directly to rest rooms, kitchens, serving equipment, and Sunday school classrooms. The latter can serve as discussion rooms, classrooms for collateral programs, or music practice rooms for the entertainers. One coffee house uses an adjoining basement room for free chess lessons: a master player and many teams are always intensely at the game while music plays in the main room.

Finally, the locating of the coffee house in the church building itself is a constant reminder to those who work there of the basis of their efforts. Not a few coffee houses located in store-fronts have had trouble remembering that it was a score of "silly irrelevant parochial congregations out in the suburbs" that paid their rent. The same lesson is available to those who come as customers. Often their experience has been limited to activities which they have long since rejected as superficial, trivial, and irrelevant. They stand to profit by the realization that some congregations *are* coming to grips with realities in the coffee houses and elsewhere.

The disadvantages of the use of church facilities are few but real. Often the selected room doubles for other church activities, so that it must be cleaned immaculately late Saturday night before Sunday school children arrive. Or, it is impossible to adequately decorate the room as a coffee house because of heavy "religious" architecture or furnishings. Related to this is the temptation of reactionary elders to baptize the room "with *some* religious symbols." Nevertheless, a number of groups caught in this predicament have managed to contrive clever ways of getting around the sentimentality without permanent damage. Moveable partitions and work counters have been invented, and Picassos have been hung directly over ancient oils of our founding fathers . . . only to be removed before the elders use the room on Sunday mornings!

This discussion of advantages and disadvantages has presupposed that certain more important and less tangible obstacles can be overcome. It may well be, for instance, that the campus intellectuals would not be caught dead in the religious foundation house or downtown church. Our assumption is that this is primarily a programmatic, rather than architectural, problem. We will deal with the programmatic aspects in Chapter Nine; suffice it here to say that there are certain matters of decoration which can make the programmatic problem easier to solve. For instance, a number of coffee houses in church buildings make use of a side or back door as the main entrance to the coffee house. Indeed, there are some downtown church parish houses to which entrance is gained by means of alleys, so that it is impossible for the visitor to know that he is seated in the basement of the church he stays away from.

In summary, there are a number of advantages and disadvantages to any choice of location. Local considerations, and especially budgets, will have to determine which option is taken. In the meantime, we can hope that a coffee house committee will be aware of the problems of any location, and try to counter them in programmatic ways.

Several items, which to the novice might seem important, have been intentionally overlooked here. Nothing has been said, for example, about the size of the room necessary. In fact, rooms of every conceivable size and shape are presently being used as coffee houses, and as common sense might lead one to suspect, smaller rooms lead to a "cozier" atmosphere for the few that can fit, while larger rooms provide a slighter degree of intimacy for a larger number of people.

The most important consideration in decoration is the way the finished product looks to the stranger. If the leaders have lived with the building for some time, they have probably forgotten about many of the distinctive features which will stand out in the eyes of others. It may be, for instance, that there is a large cross engraved in the stone arch over the back door of the church basement. Do the corridor doors carry legends like "pastor's study," "memorial gift of . . . ," or other "churchy" slogans? These often overlooked signs and symbols may be compromising to strangers who would otherwise feel open and free at the coffee house.

The general decor of the coffee house, both inside and out, will have to take into account the *Sitz im Leben* of the proposed clientele. There is only one "norm" that can be recommended, and that is that the decor be "indigenous" to the customers. College students will tolerate—or thrive on—decors which would repulse working married adults. If a number of answers to these kinds of questions are not obvious, it may be that the first task of the appropriate planning committee should be to invite typical prospective customers to sit down with them and discuss plans. One college chaplain, far removed from Greenwich Village, even sent questionnaires to a random sample of his university's students, asking what *they* thought a coffee house should look like.

If the leaders involved are not familiar with decors of the favorite hangouts of the customers they expect to serve, it is obvious that some very basic groundwork has been overlooked. Under such circumstances, the coffee house ought to be postponed at least a year, while the leadership catches up on its homework.

art for every type
of soul —
Portraits and lessons
on commission —
843 Corona
SHOES
Public health standards &
Our own Descretion ~
Behoove Our Patrons ~
Enter And Remain ~
SHOD
Live Po
TORINO

5. Equipment and Serving

The Kitchen

Possible equipment for the preparation of food and drink range from crude hot plates and paper cups to shining stainless steel soda-fountain restaurant-quality fixtures. If the coffee house can use existing "church supper" facilities, many of the major items will be supplied already. When starting from scratch, a number of factors must be kept in mind. In the first place, kitchen facilities should be comparable in quality to the rest of the coffee house. Formica tabletops demand stainless steel work counters. Otherwise, the contrast will invite criticism of one area or the other.

In the second place, kitchen facilities must be adequate for the menu. A separate coffee-making device is necessary for each kind of coffee on the menu, and heavy demand items will require heavier equipment. American coffee might require a ninety-cup electric percolator, but many places use Italian range-top espresso makers. Tea requires only one hot water source, a set of canisters for storage of the loose or bagged tea, and individual cups or pots (Japanese imported pots are cheap, attractive, and popular). Cold drinks require either adequate refrigerator space for each serving pitcher, or individual counter-top fountain-type refrigeration units (commonly seen in restaurants for noncarbonated fruit drinks). Soda pop requires refrigeration space. An alternative for cold drinks is one source of ice water and a supply of flavored syrups. Restaurant suppliers sometimes have exotic blends available by the gallon. Kool-ade is often popular in the summer.

There are three levels of food service, each requiring progressively more expensive facilities. Pastries and donuts require only a display area and napkins or paper plates. Cold sandwiches require counter working space for preparation, and refrigeration for meats and spreads. Hot sandwiches and full meals require either frying pans or full grill facilities. The more extensive menus also require better-trained kitchen workers, although simplification of the menu ("hamburgers only") minimizes this problem.

In the third place, elaborate kitchen facilities are a costly matter. If restaurant-quality equipment is used, it will prove economical only on a long-term basis. All of the better products—stainless steel, formica, and iron grills—are very expensive, even with a "church discount." On the other hand, the intentions of the coffee house may very well justify heavy expense in certain cases.

Finally, local health ordinances may require certain kinds of equipment in the kitchen, especially in the urban locations. These ordinances are usually readily available from the appropriate municipal offices, and vary widely from city to city. Application of zoning ordinances has been extremely unpredictable for coffee houses: many get by under the same approval given to the church for church suppers, while others are required to take out full restaurant licenses, or even cabaret licenses. In addition, there may be state and county licenses required.

The coffee house has not yet emerged as a distinct category of activity in the eyes of the law. The experience of many coffee houses has been that the attitude of the local police toward the social value of the coffee house has had decisive effect upon their subjective interpretation of the laws which they are called to enforce. Within limits, the legal relationship of the coffee house to the legally constituted church organization will have some effect upon the application of zoning ordinances.

The Infamous Espresso Machine has been a subject of special interest in the coffee house ministry. Because of its traditional role in the commercial coffee houses, and because of its large price tag (several hundred dollars if purchased new, and difficult to service if not), opinions are sharply divided. There are those who insist that a coffee house is not a coffee house without one, and the older or bigger the better. On the other hand, there are many who say that it isn't in the least required. An impartial analysis of the situation must conclude that an Espresso machine is a drawing card, or at least a topic of conversation where present, and never missed where it is absent.

Dishwashing equipment often presents a special problem in the kitchen. Most communities have explicit regulations about the washing and rinsing temperatures and sterilization procedures, if automatic equipment is not used. If the zoning officers do not enforce these laws, common sense demands careful attention to this detail. Where adequate washing facilities are neither provided nor procurable, modern plastic cups (of cellular construction, or disposable inserts) and paper plates might be the best choice. Paper, even coated with plastic, should never be used for hot coffee save perhaps in an emergency. Connoisseurs say that they can tell the difference, and in this case the customer is always right.

Auxiliary Equipment

Many communities have local ordinances requiring that separate toilet facilities be provided for each sex in all places which serve food. If they are not available in the desired location, the committee should bear in mind that their installation—especially in existing buildings—is very expensive. In addition, larger cities require adequate ventilation in the absence of air conditioning, and industrial exhaust fans are very expensive.

Almost all public places are subject to fire safety regulations concerning the number and kind of entrances and exits, the legal capacity of the room, and sometimes the fireproof quality of wall and floor coverings and even the furniture.

Depending upon the financial arrangements chosen, some means of collecting and recording income is necessary. A low-overhead resort-area coffee house in California has a "Gold Pan" near the door for contributions. Most rely only on some kind of "cash box," but a number use regular commercial cash registers. If waiters and waitresses are to leave guest checks, these will have to be purchased or printed.

Almost every coffee house has some kind of stage or entertainment area. In small rooms it need not be elaborate—a special chair or stool. But in larger rooms a raised platform may prove helpful. In addition, if the overall room lighting is not sufficient to read facial expressions at a distance, stage lighting is desirable. This may take the form of ordinary ceiling fixtures, or may be augmented by spotlights (such as the PAR-type at 75, 100, or 150 watts), or regular bulbs in food-can improvised shields can be made. One coffee house made footlights economically by putting a furring strip inside a ten-foot section of aluminum roof gutter. A string of Christmas tree bulbs tacked to the furring strip provided smooth illumination without shadows. Stock steel strips bent (with the aid of a propane torch) and bolted to the gutter provided legs, which were capped with rubber cane tips. When the decor permits improvisation, there are innumerable possibilities.

Even the smaller rooms will be improved with the addition of a sound system for the stage. Since music is likely desired, "high fidelity" quality is necessary in microphone, amplifier, and speakers. If it is necessary to save money here, good used equipment would be better than brand-new inferior components. In most places audio consultants will be more than glad to make extensive recommendations. Once the amplifier and speakers are provided, it is a simple matter to add a turntable, FM tuner, or tape transport. A full tape recorder connected to the system can also be used for recording the better-than-average programs for later playback. The use of stereophonic systems in places such as restaurants is vastly overrated and probably wasteful, except as a publicity trick. The sound system should be located so that it may be adjusted during programs as required without embarrassing interruptions.

The design construction and operation of these facilities provides an easy opportunity for laymen of talent and skill to contribute materially to this stage of the coffee house program. Those personally unable to meet the public may be quite able to contribute to the more mechanical aspects of the operation.

Serving and Serving Equipment

Second only to the debate over store-front or church basement is the debate over self-service or waiter service. The self-service school draws its inspiration from the folklorian image of the bartender-priest. He is the man who goes patiently about his duties on the other side of the bar until a customer engages him in conversation. Like the priest behind the altar rail, he serves the sacramental elements, occasionally hearing confession at the same time. The customers have to come to him—he will never leap over the bar to chase them save for nonpayment. The "bar" provides maximum security for the customer, therefore. He must move toward it or away, as the spirit moves him. And he always knows where to find the bartender, if he wants him.

The waiter-service school finds this relationship too limited. In the absence of a more relaxing brew, few persons "hang" on the bar. They come to it and quickly move back to the tables to drink, leaving the bartenders isolated and incommunicado. So waiters and waitresses move out among the people at the tables, taking orders, and, if invited to do so, engaging in conversation. If there are enough waiters to go around, they can even settle down for lengthier conversations when welcomed. When the waiters are free to move to the tables with their customers, it takes some of the sharp edges off their respective roles and makes communication easier.

If the "bar" style of work is accepted, display areas for food will have to be provided. Glass-topped pastry display cabinets, such as are common in bakeries, are used in the "Intersection" in San Francisco. If waiters are the pattern, then the only requirement is that the food be accessible to them, although it may also be displayed. "The Potter's House" in Washington, D. C., uses French-pastry wagons to take the evening's offerings to each table.

Cups and saucers should be appropriate to the general decor of the coffee house. It is a matter of local option whether ninety-five-cent restaurant-quality cups are used, or nine-cent discount-house specials. The cheaper ones break easier, but *not* ten times easier. Therefore, more expensive ones should be chosen only if they make a positive contribution in design or color. Where food plates are used they should be of a quality and style appropriate to the other utensils—paper does not go with china!

Between the paper plate and restaurant quality options lies a field many dollars wide. But it is possible to find good quality equipment

secondhand, either at reduced prices or as outright gifts. One coffee house received a valuable, if worn, set of silver from a large hotel that was changing its pattern. Another received the loan of a roomful of tables and chairs from a restaurant. The reception of gifts will be facilitated if the coffee house (or one of its sponsoring groups) has an obvious "charitable" identification before the law, so that the donor can write it off as a contribution for tax purposes.

ADDITIONAL INFORMATION . . .

Exotic coffee house menus are available free of charge from the Coffee Information Service, 300 East 44th Street, New York, New York 10017 (an agency of the National Coffee Association). Ask for the "Coffee House Packet."

Do It Yourself Coffee Houses, a 16-page booklet of hints and tips on mechanical details, is also available from the same source.

A handbook on mass feeding programs (available from the Federal Government) and a textbook for a chef's school (in your public library) will provide additional help.

The coffee-growing industry maintains the Pan-American Coffee Bureau in New York City. Its "Coffee Brewing Center" at 120 Wall Street provides information and advice on the most effective methods of brewing coffee. They also evaluate brewing equipment. A free "Coffee House Packet" of helpful information is available on request.

6. Finances and Resources

The following outline includes the major items of expense which should be considered:

CAPITAL EXPENSES:

1. Renovation of the coffee house rooms
2. Furniture: tables and chairs, lounges
3. Kitchen: preparation and storage facilities
4. Stage and related equipment
5. Tableware: cups, saucers, plates, accessories

OPERATING EXPENSES:

1. Rental of property
2. Manager or director's salary
3. Janitorial services
4. Food supplies
5. Utilities
6. Publicity and program materials

Renovation of rooms must include not only zoning and licensing requirements, but interior decoration according to the motif of the coffee house. It may be possible to save here by using student or parish handymen either entirely or in cooperation with skilled tradesmen (if the building code permits).

Furniture which is purchased new is very expensive. According to reports, used furniture is often contributed, and homemade varieties not only save money but unite the volunteers in enjoyable work parties. Used living-room furniture donated by parishioners may even be preferable to new, since it will be used hard by many persons who will not treat it with "churchy" respect.

The opposite is true of the kitchen: new, restaurant-quality equipment will provide better service in every department. Most home-quality equipment is not built to take continuous heavy usage. Volunteers will work hard enough with adequate equipment: their job should not be compounded by improvisation in the kitchen. If good equipment is available from the existing church dining room, it will save money. But if it must be returned to some other place each week, it will hardly be worth the savings.

Stage facilities, including both lights and sound, can be very expensive. Sound equipment may be procured at great savings in kit form from some of the larger electronic supply houses, or "used" from hi-fi enthusiasts who have stepped up to stereo. Authentic stage-lighting equipment is within reach, if it can be secured second-hand from the local repertory theatre or university drama department, who sometimes have outdated equipment which they will part with for charity or a small price.

Tableware can be purchased, often at a "church discount" from a restaurant supplier, who will also give credit terms. But a much smaller cash outlay will procure inexpensive Japanese cups and saucers which break easily but are easily replaced. Any pattern will have to be a compromise among aesthetics, utility, and cost.

By far the biggest expense is usually room rental, at least in the store-front situation. This expense is compounded by the problems of leases, deposits, and guarantees. Rental is a fixed item, which cannot usually be adjusted according to patronage as the other operating expenses can. (But sometimes the threat of a six months' lease forces a coffee house committee to achieve a desirable maturity before launching the boat.)

The second big item in operating expenses is the manager or director's salary. Where the person who fills this role is already on the staff of the sponsoring organization, it is easy to overlook the cost. But every coffee house has found it necessary to have at least one paid person who assumes direct responsibility for the details of daily operation. With volunteer staffs, it is inevitable that every once in a while the minister in charge will have to brew the coffee or sweep the floors; there must be someone who will be liable for blame, and who can represent the group before boards and agencies.

His primary responsibility may be a clerical one: the training of the saints for their service in the coffee house ministry. In some cases, the professional handles the "cleaner" responsibilities, while a part-time student takes care of cleaning and locking the doors. In such situations, the "janitor" is paid directly out of the proceeds, while the professional is paid from the regular budget of the sponsoring agency. In several places, a seminarian is hired specifically to direct the coffee house, under the supervision of the regular minister or agency representative.

The cost of food supplies varies directly with the consumption, minus waste. Tea and syrups are easy to keep, but a large percolator full of coffee is worthless at closing time. Donuts and pastries loose much of their appeal the second day, and a sandwich spread spoils quickly. A good source of information in this area is a friendly cook at the neighborhood restaurant. He may also direct one to his wholesalers for good supplies.

Utilities are a fixed operating expense. A pay telephone located right in the coffee house will save abuse of the office phone, especially if teenagers (who must call home for a ride) frequent.

Publicity can be needlessly expensive. For the coffee house, the best advertisement is by word of mouth. If a great deal of money seems necessary to draw people into the coffee house, the trouble probably lies in what happens to them once they get inside. But program materials and personnel should not cost money, either. If it is necessary to pay performers, one might better frequent the commercial coffee houses instead. What is "good" about many coffee houses is not that they are cheap places to hear "name" folk singers, but that they present seemingly ordinary persons with creative talents who are not solicited by or attracted to the commercial show-business world. (Even the most confirmed coffee house aficionados will have to admit that something was lost when record companies invaded the Village and rebellion became lucrative.)

Every noncommercial coffee house depends upon one or more forms of subsidy. In its most common form, this subsidy consists of both direct appropriations from the sponsoring church or organization budget, and a financial fluidity which amounts to "loans." Inclusion in the overall budget can provide enough flexibility to cover capital outlay in the fall, with net income during the year paying back a part of the "loan."

The second level of support comes in the appeal to additional churches in the area for direct contributions to the budget. Sometimes this is done individually, sometimes through the local Council of Churches. Where this is not tried, it is usually because there is fear of control of unfavorable influence over the programmatic freedom of the coffee house. The validity of this fear can only be judged by those involved in each local situation; but a number of places have shown that "interpretation" is possible. With several Protestant denominations now issuing program materials about coffee houses, it would appear that the job of interpretation may become easier in the future.

Business and industry may be potential sources of support, especially where the base of organization is increasingly ecumenical. In some locations a dominating business has been convinced that the coffee house would make a contribution to the social welfare of all persons, in spite of sectarian sponsorship.

The denominations are making sizable investments in certain experimental ministries, such as "Intersection" coffee house in San Francisco and the strip ministry in Las Vegas. The coffee house ministries should now be documented sufficiently to receive the same kinds of financial help that are available to congregations for other projects. Denominational program materials are already available from at least two denominations, and others will soon follow suit.

Only one coffee house, "The Center," in Jackson, Wyoming, owes its existence to the concern and generosity of a single benefactor, but in several others a number of individual laymen have made financial sacrifices, either in the form of gifts of cash and equipment, or by taking on the uninsured debt of the capital expenses.

In addition to the subsidy mentioned above, every coffee house has some source of current income. This may be a cover charge, ranging from ten cents to a dollar, either in lieu of or in addition to charges for individual menu items. Entrées may be priced over a wide range, depending on other charges and the customer's willingness to pay. American coffee, for instance, may

be given away, or go for anywhere from five to fifty cents a cup. Indeed, all of the various means of financing such church activities have been tried (memberships, drag-stag admission differential, etc.).

Two unique sources of income for the coffee house are profits from the sale of paperback books (purchased, at discount, directly from the publisher) and commissions on the sale of paintings and photography on display there (usually about ten percent).

Nonprofit Coffee Houses

We have used the term "nonprofit" in the technical sense, inasmuch as no individual receives personal profit from the business. But most coffee houses are nonprofit in the descriptive sense, as well. Usually those coffee houses which are housed in church-owned facilities, directed by regular church staff, with only moderate expenses for renovation (e.g., less than $1,000), are able to show a modest "gain" which can be applied toward improvements or program expenses, and thus help to improve the quality of the activity in the coffee house. But we are not aware of any coffee house which must pay overhead expenses directly that is not heavily subsidized by a church or group of churches. We are not, of course, speaking here of commercial coffee houses. Some "legitimate" coffee houses probably show a modest profit, but many have been forced to close.

It may be that the coffee house of modest investment may replace the church bazaar as a combination social affair and fund-raising device. In a number of campus ministry coffee houses, the overhead expenses are paid out of the general budget, while net profit finances many related campus ministry projects.

Part Three: Brewing a Coffee House

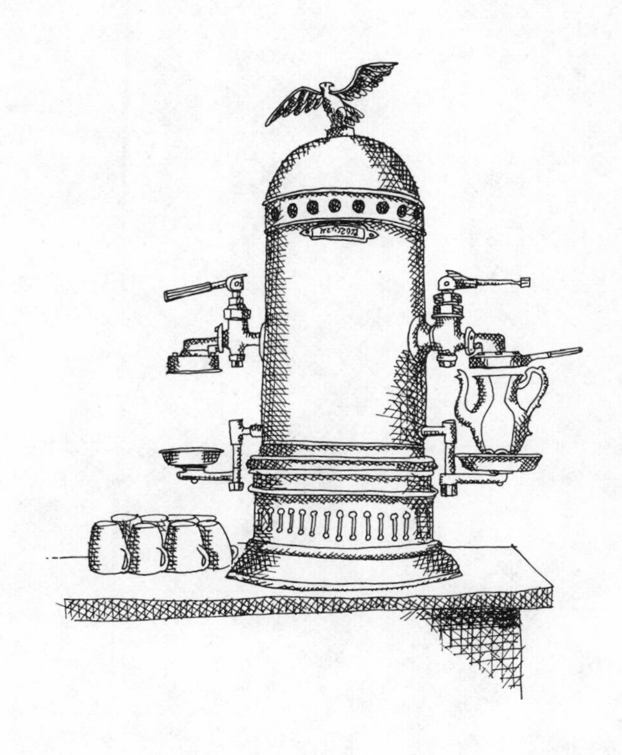

7. Sponsors and Managers

We have been using the term "church-related coffee house" rather indiscriminately throughout to refer to the relationship between the church and coffee house. There are two basic options.

The Church-Sponsored Coffee House

The elementary form of the relationship is direct church sponsorship. This form provides the easiest way to "get off the ground," the simplest organization, and the most direct control over the destiny of the operation.

The church-sponsored coffee house is organizationally similar and parallel to all the other church activity groups: it is a committee of church members responsible to the church's governing board; it gains its legal existence from the church governing board just as the Ladies' Aid or Boy Scout troop. As such, it enjoys the same rights to the use of church facilities as the other groups (including the right to draw upon the pastor's time and energies) and usually receives some or all of its finances by appropriation from the annual budget. The church may decide to decorate one or more of its rooms or basement in harmony with the plans of the coffee house committee, just as it provides a ladies' parlor or youth room. It may also be eligible to enjoy effective short-term loans, in the form of internal transactions with the church treasury, in order to purchase supplies before income starts to come in, or it may use the church's credit rating to the same end.

The church-sponsored coffee house does not necessarily have

to meet in the church basement, although this option is often taken. Apparently the same factors which make a group take the basement location often also persuade them to take this closer form of sponsorship, although there is no necessary connection.

The Church-Related Type

We are using the term "church-related" to include a wide range of possible relationships which are less direct than formal organic sponsorship by a local church. The essential characteristic is the organic autonomy of the coffee house committee, which often includes legal incorporation. This does not preclude a very close relationship to one local church, but it includes the possibility of additional relationship to other local churches, as well as civic organizations.

The "related" organization is considerably more on its own to secure and maintain facilities, a balanced budget, staff, and internal coherence. At the same time, it enjoys a greater degree of organizational and programmatic freedom than is possible when the group is directly responsible to a board of trustees or vestry. Such coffee houses are able to schedule programs on controversial topics without committing any particular church to a viewpoint and without running the risk of censorship. (The risk of misunderstanding is always present!)

It should be obvious that neither the "sponsored" nor the "related" form of organization enjoys any unqualified advantage over the other, and presence of or absence of local factors must be taken into consideration.

The Organization

It is certainly possible to proceed without any formal organization to the coffee house, and rely solely upon the charismatic appeal and behind-the-scenes maneuvering ability of a single "director" or "chairman." Although the one-man show does enable a more responsive coffee house, considered on a short-term basis it suffers from several setbacks over a period of time.

The first and most obvious limitation is the problem of horizontal mobility. With an average American residency of five years, the chances are even that any given director or leader will move before two and a half years pass. If he has been running the show himself, continuity will be a major problem. The second limitation imposed by the absence of a clearly defined organization sharing responsibility has cropped up all too frequently in coffee houses. We can call it the "in-group syndrome." In practice, a group of persons gravitate into positions of favor with the leader, so that they win his confidence and begin to participate in decision-making processes. Having thus achieved a position of power, they jealously guard their achieved status by seeking to prevent others from doing the same thing. Thus it becomes impossible for new persons—who might have creative contributions to make—to penetrate the in-group's shell. In this encounter, the in-group spends an increasing amount of energy protecting itself against outsiders, with the result that programming—and the coffee house—decay for want of creativity. Of course, this interpersonal dynamic operates in many other activities, but it has emerged as a special problem in many coffee houses, apparently because of the absence of historical patterns. In seeking to avoid the problems of the "pecking order" of the Ladies' Aid power structure, a new problem has emerged.

The corrective is a clearly defined organization. It may be simple: a committee of several persons appointed by the minister, or elected by the membership of the youth work committee or other initiating group. In more complex form, it may require a complete organizational chart, with a central committee composed of delegates elected by sponsoring churches, and a dozen subcommittees. There are a number of options in between these extremes, depending upon the ambitiousness of the undertaking. A written constitution is almost essential, to divide responsibilities and fix the blame, to prevent future chaos. For the "related" type, some means of limiting personal liability—usually incorporation as a nonprofit corporation, or, where the state laws permit, as an educational foundation—should be seriously considered.

The Coffee House Manager

The governing committee will want to designate officers, including at least a chairman to convene meetings and a treasurer to handle the books. The first task of the committee, once the organizational details have been settled, will be the designation or appointment of a "manager" or "director" for the coffee house, with power and authority to carry out policy decisions. This may be the minister or his assistant, or a part-time seminarian hired just for this purpose. In certain applications, a layman trained for the job would be appropriate. Many activities of churches are able to proceed without complications from one meeting of the governing committee to another, but there are so many contingent problems that arise in an evening's operation of the coffee house, that a designated officer is essential. It is impossible to wait until the next monthly board meeting to decide what to do about the leaky coffeepot or broken sound system.

The qualifications for the manager's post are simple: he must be, first of all, a theological specialist, who is able to relate and interpret the historic task of the church into concrete marketplace realities in the ongoing education and reflection of the coffee house committee. He must be an administrator of the highest qualifications, to keep the whole operation running smoothly. The Ladies' Aid will wait while Mrs. Smith fumbles through the hymnal looking for a fellowship song, but coffee house customers will get justifiably irritated if their program is slovenly run. One volunteer made ninety cups of clear coffee in an electric percolator in four minutes! No one could figure out what was wrong, until the manager discovered that she started with boiling water. The manager must be an expert with the sound system and stage lighting, able to back up the volunteers. He must be a practicing psychologist, able to interpret the rivalries between kitchen workers and turn hostilities into constructive activity. He must be adept at sweeping floors, for those evenings when the volunteers all mysteriously disappear just at closing time. Finally, he must be a man of considerable faith, to keep a cool head, warm heart, and open mind in the midst of continuous physical labor and unpredictable interpersonal confrontations.

Since it is impossible to find a sane human being who would wish this upon himself, he must be paid, in humility, just as a congregation pays its theological expert to preach and teach. The leadership of a coffee house committee is as demanding a clerical ministry as any other—perhaps even more so, because there is no tradition to fall back on.

Purpose and Direction

It falls upon the sponsoring group and its committee to provide the basic statements of purpose of the coffee house, and to set the tone for working out a philosophy for the achievement of the agreed purposes. For some this will seem to be a perfectly natural step. But there are many persons who are called into the coffee house ministry who rebel against "purposes" as somehow subversive of genuine human relationships within the coffee house. These persons see statements of purpose as indications of institutionality and, therefore, of corruption.

There is little that we can offer such persons, except pity and the thought that, in the absence of a conscientious statement of purpose, the coffee house will of necessity operate on the multitude of unspoken and unexamined purposes of those who participate. It is naïve to expect that these private purposes will automatically dovetail into a harmonious whole. A number of coffee houses have been strained by the unhappy conflict of diverse and incompatible purposes. In the process of arriving at a common purpose, it may be expected that many individuals' private and personal motives will be subjugated to the common good; many volunteers, for instance, will become sufficiently impressed with the common goal that they begin to work for it, forsaking their own selfish motives in the process or finding ways to combine their personal motives with the group's.

The unlimited possibilities of conflicting motives, even among the most dedicated volunteers, should immediately remind us that the task of reflection, evaluation, and discussion of the coffee house purpose is a never-ending one, which cannot be discharged in a single mass meeting at the beginning of the year. It falls upon the sponsors to ensure that this task is not neglected.

Whether the coffee house is church-sponsored or church-related, it is important that those who are ultimately footing the bill pay serious attention to the ability of the coffee house to achieve those measurable ends for which it was set up. In a day when the church is confronted by countless worthy projects, the coffee house ministry can only be operated by sacrificing some other mission. One coffee house manager declared recently, "It is almost impossible for anyone to judge the success of the coffee house ministry." He was thinking in terms of the effect of the coffee house on the lives of the people it serves, and, in view of our discussion in Chapter One, he was certainly right. But he overlooked a number of lesser tests which we can—and should—apply to the coffee house ministry.

Participation in the coffee house ministry should produce a number of discernible effects in the lives of the volunteers and managers. In the first place, it should lead to a radical open-mindedness toward different religious traditions and theological systems. This follows naturally from the program goals.

In the second place, participation should lead to an increase in ecumenical fervor. This is a result of an appreciation for and understanding of our separated brethren, gained through conversation with them in the coffee house. In the third place, it should produce a desire to learn more and more about one's own religious tradition and theology. When confronted by persons with better-developed theological minds, most laymen are startled to realize that they do not even know what it is that they are supposed to believe.

In the fourth place, it should lead to an increased participation in the traditional life of the church, especially in the liturgy. As nominal Christians become involved, sometimes for the first time, in a mission project, they are forced to take more seriously their own dependence on the institutionalized means of grace. Finally, that distinctively Christian quality of fellowship, *koinonia,* should be manifest in the corporate lives of the workers. *Koinonia* is not generically related to, and has nothing to do with, smiling. It is not based on likemindedness, but derives from the disciples' awareness of their separate sinfulness and common Savior.

If a search for the above characteristics among the workers proves successful, then and only then can the sponsors begin to hope for signs from the community which is served by the coffee house. We cannot necessarily expect any increase in church membership rolls, or any new converts to the Lord. This may happen, and it may not. That is not our concern; it is a matter between God and them. What we can reasonably expect are indications that the world begins to understand what it is that the church is proclaiming. In the early stages, we may expect the world to be puzzled by this activity of the church. The old stereotypes—moralism and absolutism—will no longer fit neatly, and many will be threatened, or at least shaken, by observations and rumors which they cannot pigeonhole. Those outside the church will ask, "What happened to the good old-time religion (which I rejected in my youth)?" When these things come to pass, we will know that the ground has been cleared for the church to begin to communicate with the world in the coffee house.

The second stage follows quickly. People will pass from puzzlement to outrage. Religious souls may well be affronted by the service of the coffee house, while liberated persons will consider our service to be folly. But there will be many who rush to defend that coffee house as a wonderful place which has brought new life to the old world. When that day comes, we will know that we have finally gotten on the track. And we will find ourselves beginning to understand the Paul of First Corinthians 1.

These signs, when they are found, are signs that the coffee house is performing its ministry faithfully. We have as much right to expect to see them in the coffee house mission as we have a right to see cured patients walk out of the medical missionary station.

There is one other sign that we may look for in the coffee house ministry. If we can continue our analogy with biblical times, we may rightfully expect that somewhere along the line, someone is going to get crucified. This author is personally aware of two young ministers who, along with their wives and families, have suffered abuse and finally dismissal for getting involved in this radical ministry. There have probably been more, but then a disciple cannot be above his Teacher. "It is enough for the disciple to be like his teacher" (Matt. 10:24).

8. The Volunteer Staff and Their Training

About five percent of the church-related coffee houses pay their staff of waiters and waitresses on a scale comparable with other restaurants in the neighborhood. They argue that this is the only way to ensure an efficient and reliable crew to operate the coffee house. That this is simply not true is testified by the other ninety-five percent. Apparently the advantages of the legal responsibility engendered by pay are outweighed by the zealous enthusiasm of those who serve solely because of the intangible spiritual, psychological, and social benefits of the volunteer system. The fact remains that there are no coffee houses with a substantial training program for volunteers that have any trouble getting workers. (A few places which weekly enlist volunteers from among the customers report a constant turnover and very low efficiency.)

The problem of the volunteer staff approach is to get sufficient *commitment* to the coffee house and its goals. There will usually be no problem getting *interest:* everybody thinks that a coffee house is a good idea, a great place, a lot of fun. It is. But it is also a lot of work for those who perform the service there. More interest will bring many customers to the coffee house, but it will hold few workers there. So the major task in organizing the volunteer staff is engendering commitment.

Nor is mere "religious" commitment sufficient to ensure the successful life of the volunteer. No matter how devoted a person may be to Jesus Christ as a Savior, the work of the coffee house will soon become overburdening unless that person is also and particularly committed to Jesus Christ the suffering servant. Many "Christians" are quite devoted to the Christ of the cross—so long as the cross remains on the altar. We have all become accustomed to cheap grace, in Bonhoeffer's terms. And even those among us who are willing to work for the Lord would rather work at tasks which are rewarding—either in terms of immediate response (who doesn't enjoy the thankfulness of orphans at Christmas parties?), or in terms of historical validation (can *anyone* doubt that teaching Sunday school is good in the eyes of the Lord?).

There is no special rationale, no private theology, of the coffee house ministry. It grows out of the same theological convictions and missionary concerns that have been abundantly talked and written about in the church in recent years. The openness of the coffee house encounter is the same openness that we are learning to cultivate even in our foreign missions. The concern for the total person—spirit, mind, and body—is the same total concern that underlies the church's involvement in civil rights and foreign policy. The dynamics of the volunteer relationship are the same dynamics that operate in every "small group" activity.

Despite the theoretical similarity of coffee house theology to theology in general, we cannot assume that volunteers know or appreciate the task. We must accept the gross illiteracy of the Christian layman today, and develop educational experiences which will meet this need. It is unlikely that many churches will be willing or able to adopt the good example of the Church of The Savior, which makes two years of basic theological education prerequisite to serving in their coffee house mission. But it is not unrealistic to ask that some theological education precede participation in the coffee house. We may draw an analogy from the preparation of the clergy, where an undergraduate degree is required for admission to seminaries. A person who attempted to gain a full theological education without such preparation would soon be overwhelmed. In the same way, a person who attempted to understand his ministry in the coffee house without first having a basic grasp of Christian thought in general would have a difficult time understanding his ministry.

On the other hand, a good argument can be made for a concept of on-the-job training in the ministry of the laity. Does a Christian education *have* to precede participation in ministry and mission? We might even ask if a Christian education *can* precede participation in ministry and mission. American theological education, in particular, has always stressed the importance of simultaneous field work and classroom study. An experimental program at Yale Divinity School even provides a half-and-half proportion in one year. It may be that the concept of the suffering servant, for instance, cannot really be understood apart from participation in it.

On the basis of such arguments, the theological education of the laity must be placed in the context of missionary activity. This does follow the model suggested by Søren Kierkegaard. In *For Self-Examination* (and elsewhere) he cautions against the idea that one might first understand the whole of God's Word, and then begin to follow it. Instead, he says, one who desires to become a Christian ought to find one thing that is required, and do it. His point is that understanding the whole is not necessary for participation in it. By the same token, one does not have to have a whole theological system under one's belt to minister to the customers of the coffee house. We might remember that Jesus' first disciples followed him faithfully for over two years before he ever asked them if they understood who he was. And the ensuing material from the confession at Caesarea Philippi make it plain that the disciples understood the idea of the Messiah, but failed to grasp the dynamic implications—the crucifixion. Our seminaries are still confronted with persons who "understand" theology in an academic way, but do not grasp the dynamic implications for their lives. On the basis of this discussion, it appears that there is some precedent for on-the-job training in the ministry of the church.

Regardless of the general theological competence of the lay volunteers participating, it does take special training to enable them to appreciate the specific application of theological truths to the new coffee house ministry. Even more importantly, they must learn to share the inspiration of those who already believe in this approach to ministry; it will not come automatically. There must be some form of training program—more or less formal—to educate the volunteers into their new experience. This training program must involve not only education into the objective nature of the task at hand, but also education into the subjective involvement of the volunteers themselves. We can single out four specific areas of this education, although in practice they will blend into one another.

1. *Discipline:* The volunteer program itself should be a model of discipline, including a commitment of time to preparation. Whether this be a weekend retreat in the fall and again in the spring, or an hour of preparation before work each evening, or somewhere in between, depends in part on local conditions—and in part upon the willingness of the leadership to prepare a substantial training program. The external discipline is but a reminder of the internal discipline that pervades the rest of the volunteer's role. The coffee house is not simply a place for frustrated church women to sit and gab as they might on the telephone. A serious, albeit often enjoyable and enlightening, ministry is to be performed here. The customers are real people, with real problems, real creativity, and real joy to share and receive.

2. *Theological Education:* The basic task of the volunteer training program is theological education. This is in part because of the overwhelming theological illiteracy of our churchmen, and in part because the coffee house provides a new on-the-job dimension to the educational process even for those quite theologically literate. It is one thing to sit around in a church parlor and discuss Jesus' washing the disciples' feet. It is quite another thing to discuss it in the coffee house kitchen while the dishwashing machine is filling for the evening's work. It is one thing to discuss the beatitudes of the meek while wearing Sunday-best clothes, and quite another when dressed for work. Discipleship takes on a new dimension when service is only a few minutes away, and healing miracles suddenly become interesting when sick and lonely people are standing outside the door waiting for the coffee house to open.

But do we understand what it is we are trying to do, and why? Our easy answers begin to fade when real life situations crop forth in all their human reality. "Love thy neighbor" was so easy, until the neighbor sat down across the table.

There is no special theological training program which is unique to the coffee house. Depending upon local conditions, all of the various study books designed for laymen's groups are appropriate, although timing may make certain books more immediately relevant. It would be dangerous to spend too much emphasis on any one group of theological motifs, such as "service" or "fellowship." A balanced program may, with patience, open unforeseen doors of discussion and insight. Unfortunately, no one has yet developed a comprehensive theological education program specifically for the coffee house ministry. Working one out will be a creative challenge for the clergy in charge.

3. *Psychological Understanding:* With the possibility of deep and intimate conversation, and the constant personal revelations that come through them, it is important that volunteers have some understanding of basic psychological processes, especially the dynamics of prejudice, psychology of religion, and personality theory—including not only objective knowledge, but subjective appreciation for their own neuroses and idiosyncrasies.

Good training material for this area can be found in course books and reading books in the field of pastoral and clinical counseling. The object is not to make amateur psychologists out of volunteers, but precisely the opposite—to show them their limitations, and teach them to recognize when conversations enter potentially dangerous areas. In understanding their own psychological makeups, the volunteers will be less likely to be a burden to the customers, and perhaps free enough from themselves to minister.

4. *Sociological Training:* In recent years a new discipline—small group dynamics—has emerged which provides no trifling help to the coffee house volunteers. A good coffee house training program might well include not only theory but practice in role play situations of various kinds. A "T" group or sensitivity-training weekend—lead by a competent specialist—can take the edge off the whole volunteer relationship problem and equip them to apply the remainder of training in constructive ways. Sensitivity training is doubtless one of the biggest problems in the communication process of the coffee house.

Role play situations in the coffee house training program are legion. Richard Mawson, Las Vegas Strip chaplain, has used them to bridge the gap between ordinary churchmen and the highly professionalized people who work the strip. Vocation specialization has become a serious barrier to communication, largely because we do not yet know how to cope with it.

Whether the various elements of the training program are presented in parallel ways, or in distinctly different parts of the course of training depends more on the ability of qualified leadership than any inherent right. They may be combined into a single hour every evening, as for instance, at the famous "Potter's House" in Washington. There a typical "hour" opened with theological discussion—Bible reading and meditation. Next came a period of Quaker silence, for reflection and meditation. Then discussion of a popular layman's book on psychology of religion. Finally, there was a period of sociological discussion, of the encounters and relationships of the previous week's work.

On the other hand, these elements may be presented sequentially, over the course of a semester; or one element or another may be stressed in a weekend retreat. At more theologically oriented coffee houses (such as "The Encounter," near Lancaster Theological Seminary in Pennsylvania), the theological side of the education comes in the content of various public programs, which are open to customers as well.

Like any other church-run program, it is easy in the coffee house to become so bogged down in mundane details that little time is taken out for reflection. But precisely because there are so few traditional ways of coffee house ministry, it is all the more important that serious and comprehensive reflection be structured into the program. It may be permissible, for instance, to seriously review the Christian education program of the church only annually. But, lacking clear directions and much experience, a coffee house program could get far afield of original—or subsequent—intentions in a few short weeks.

The Form of the Training

In a generation where "the missionary structure of the congregation" has become a password in avant-garde thinking about the nature of the church, it hardly seems necessary to bring up the form of the training program. Needless to say, the form of the training hour (or weekend) will have at least as much influence upon the volunteers as the content.

A presentation which is not dialogical will not engender dialogue in the coffee house. If the object of the training is to prepare volunteers for "communication" in their work, it will itself have to be a model of sensitivity and openness. This does *not* mean that every training session has to be an unstructured bull session, for, as Reuel Howe says, even a lecture can be dialogical. It does mean that there are no authoritarian shortcuts to staff training.

There is another reason why the training program's form is so important. If what we have intimated about the essential sinful similarity of the servers and the served is true, any training program which delves into deep discussion will reveal the same concerns and problems in the volunteers that they will later find in the customers. The way in which things like confession are handled in the training session will become for the volunteers the model for their relationships with the customers. If the volunteers are superficial with each other, they will probably be the same with their customers.

On the other hand, the aspect of the on-the-job training will add a rich possibility to the training program's opportunities. It may be that the volunteers will not learn to confess their sins to one another until they have recognized this same confession on the lips of their customers.

Finally, the training program itself needs to become a channel and means of grace. This may involve full and formal communion service at the beginning or end of the training hour or weekends. It may take the form of an unspoken but meaningful sharing of coffee and donuts by the volunteers before or after the evening's work. But somewhere along the course of the evening the volunteers need to become conscious of receiving and depending upon the gift of God's grace to enable them to carry out their ministry.

In view of the function of the training program as a model for the whole evening's work, it may not be best to use traditional sectarian service; on the other hand, properly interpreted, the

traditional liturgy has the advantage of familiarity. In either case, the interpretation of the service is at least as important as the service itself. If the Word does convey grace as efficaciously as the Sacrament in the theology of the sponsors and participants, the form of the training program should take this into account. On the other hand, the meaning of sacrament has become greatly intensified for many free churchmen when it consists of leftover donuts and coffee at the end of a hard evening's work.

FLY TWA
SUPERJETS
SAS
HANSA

9. Programming the Coffee House

In essence a coffee house is nothing more—or less—than a container for a program. Without it, the coffee house is only a coffee shop, a small restaurant. All of the preparation, decoration, and calculation have their end in the presentation in the coffee house of a "program" of one kind or another.

In terms of the investment of time and energy of the sponsors, the coffee house is an alternative to organizing a "club" or activity group or perhaps even a lecture series. But the coffee house does not eliminate these activities, it merely adds to the possibilities for them. Strictly speaking, the coffee house is only an alternative to an empty auditorium or parlor. All the activities which formerly would have been put on in such rooms can now be done better in the coffee house setting.

Traditional activities like lectures and other formal programs have been adopted in the past by churches without any serious consideration of the applicability of the form to the kind of message which the church tries to communicate to the world. Now for the first time it is possible to raise the question whether the church can honestly and consciously sponsor a formal lecture. A formal lecture, delivered to listeners deployed in rows beneath the speakers' platform implies certain relationships which may in fact be contrary to the point of our message. Professor X has every right to pontificate on the theory of relativity to students who enroll in his course. They know that he is the authority and they elect to listen. Does the church, on the other hand, really want to proclaim "good news" in this formal and authoritarian manner? We do that often now, but do we really want to? Do we have any other choice?

In the coffee house we do have an alternative. The informality of the small-tables-and-chairs setting, emphasized by the possibility of eating, drinking, and smoking during the course of a lecture, concert, or program, takes the authoritarian edge off the presentation. No one need feel that the speaker's rostrum demands any more attention than he is freely willing to give it. If you don't like the talk, you can doodle on your tablecloth, thumb through a paperback, or quietly drink your coffee. You can come and go as you please. The coffee house setting gives considerably more personal freedom and, therefore, integrity to the persons present.

The informality operates also after a presentation has been made. Where the speaker is elevated to a position of formal prominence by the structure of the auditorium, it takes a certain amount of courage and perhaps even hostility to direct a question to the "authority" on stage. Even if he is a congenial chap, he possesses great power to offend or squelch a questioner. Honest disagreement is at best a dangerous business because of this power differential.

The problem is greatly reduced in the coffee house. After a chat from the stage (punctuated by the continual tinkling of spoons and the shuffling of chairs), the speaker of the evening may entertain a few questions, usually of clarification. Then he moves to a "discussion table" where interested parties may join him for deeper exploration of the topic. There is a kind of equality over coffee cups that permits and even encourages dialogical discussion.

In a similar manner, the coffee house enjoys certain distinct advantages over the informal program forms. Small group discussions are becoming increasingly popular in the churches. Their basic limitation comes from their reputation for intimacy. Few people are willing to become involved in a small group, such as a *koinonia* group or Bible study class, unless they are convinced ahead of time that it will be relatively safe to do so.

As a result, a degree of in-groupishness is requisite to beginning. The participants of practical necessity share certain minimal external similarities—they may be members of the same church, dormitory, or organization. For example, a certain Wesley Club

(Methodist student group) decided that they should wrestle with the "new morality on campus" in a discussion. No one present could even begin to explain the basis of the new morality, let alone try to defend it. The regulars found their Thou-shalt-not ethic confirmed by each other, and, satisfied of their virtue, returned to dormitories half full of nonvirgins. There had been no dialogue, nor even any deep discussion. The church had completely failed to bring any good news to the campus that night. A topic that might well have profited from dialogue was cast in the wrong setting.

One of the most promising aspects of the coffee house ministry is that all of the standard program forms can and have been employed there, with great success. Approximately half of all coffee house formal programming involves folk singing. Second in popularity is poetry reading, taking another quarter. The remaining quarter of the programs include lectures, speeches, movies, debates, discussions, plays, dramatic readings, and instrumental concerts (trios, small ensembles, etc.). But this overall proportion does not take into account the fact that some coffee houses have all folk singing, and others have none. Some have only folk singing, and others have only a little of it. The proportions at any given coffee house vary considerably, depending upon the program goals and clientele.

A good many coffee houses have a "daily" system. One night of the week is given over to one kind of program, the next to another. Friday night may always be folk singing night, Saturday is jazz, Sunday is classical music, and Monday is poetry night. (Those who use this system usually have a corresponding rotation of volunteer staffs.)

Program Goals

Various programs and program forms can be employed to achieve a variety of program goals at the same time. In many instances these goals will be at least as important as the "content" of the program. The encouragement of *creativity* is probably the most universal goal of any coffee house operation. Coffee houses draw upon kinds of creativity which are not often elicited by other agencies of society. Church-related coffee houses, which do not consider the box-office criterion as primary qualification, are in a position to exercise even greater freedom to respond to potential expressions of the creative spirit.

Among college students the universal "gripe" is often the impersonality of mass society. Without attempting to adjudicate the theological problem, we can offer the judgment that the coffee house is able to provide a new and accessible outlet for "self-expression." A number of persons have inquired of the regional and national sources of good programs, not realizing that many good programs exist in their own neighbors! The individualistic element of modern dance crazes is testimony to backlog of individual expression of talents and interests which may not be "marketable" elsewhere.

"Stimulation" or "challenge" is a frequent goal of coffee house programming. The assumption, not very farfetched, is that many groups lack local involvement in the big issues of our day. The coffee house is one way to bridge the information gap in an entertaining manner.

An African student may be invited to speak on problems of the developing nations; a favorite professor might speak on international tensions. Or, local issues can be treated in a new light: a graduate student once read a short story which raised questions about campus morals, and a prison warden spoke of inmate conditions. The variety of forms which may be employed (lecture, musical, or dramatic presentation, etc.) permit each issue to be raised in the most provocative and productive way. The object of such presentations is usually to stimulate a deeper level of table conversation after the formal program is concluded. The waiters and waitresses and other in-group members, alerted to the topic, may begin conversations in the absence of customers' initiative.

A hybrid form of stimulation is the goal of "communication" or "dialogue" *between polar groups.* In every social situation there are groups which are not in communication—students and faculty, faculty and staff, Negroes and whites, town and gown, conservative and liberal, boys and girls. Through calculated invitations of both customers and performers, it is often possible to provide an opportunity for these alienated factions to sit down together—sometimes for the first time.

Of course, it should be obvious that left to their natural instincts, people will not come into situations which will be threatening. A number of coffee houses have found that it is not enough to get people there—once they come, something must be done to keep them coming back. We are not suggesting that techniques and gimmicks which deny the customers' humanity be employed. We are suggesting one of the prime tasks confronting a coffee house is the creation of an atmosphere of acceptance which will permit people to return, even if their pride is not always flattered.

The advertising world operates on the assumption that it is moral to appeal primarily to people's human needs and wants. "Feature yourself driving this sleek new sports car," the ads say. "Give your ego a boost." The church's assumptions, on the other hand, are decidedly different. We assume that certain exaggerated human needs are the result of unfulfilled spiritual needs, or, to use traditional jargon, that sins are the result of sin. We do not treat the symptoms, but the cause. In the coffee house, then, we are not simply offering to do what the world does better. We are offering a climate of acceptance which does not depend on flattery or even the ego-boosting benefits of association with like-minded people. (Although, we hasten to confess, that we are unable to completely divest ourselves of these worldly gimmicks is a sign of our little faith.)

Indeed, the greatest problem confronting the coffee house ministry and the church today is to learn, or discover, how to create the theologically correct atmosphere of acceptance without the offensiveness of sectarian paraphernalia. Dietrich Bonhoeffer's *Life Together,* for instance, is a provocative discussion of the nature of Christian community, and can profitably be studied by coffee house committees. But it was written to encourage a Christian minority persecuted by the Nazis on the eve of World War II. It sought an identifiable and orthodox Christian piety which was very appropriate at that time, but definitely is not today. Bonhoeffer himself, some six years later, anticipated the problems of our pluralistic, post-Christian era—but he did not live to update his thoughts on the nature of the church under such circumstances. He summarily predicted that by this time the "form of the church will have changed beyond recognition." It hasn't, but we are trying.

On the other hand, Harvey Cox's best seller, *The Secular City,* represents a serious attempt to come to grips with the changed world that Bonhoeffer predicted. He does make many interesting observations on the relationship between certain theological affirmations and the findings of the social sciences. But merely understanding the secular city will not, in itself, help us to become effective servants of Christ in it. Bridging the gap between the sectarian church and the secular city is still a task before us, and it will not help to simply replace the one with the other as Cox does. We do not want to capitulate to either the past or the present; we want to know how to minister in the future.

The only lasting resolution of this theological problem requires that we work with all the givens. We must find a way to maintain theologically partisan viewpoints in a pluralistic world. Under such a system, an authentic pluralism would be defined to include the essential right of each viewpoint to contribute to theological discussion. It has been said that all religions are to their adherents equally true, to the philosophers equally false, and to the magistrates equally useful. What we are doing is removing the cynical relativity: all religions are, in fact, equally true, false, and useful. Since all religions are human creations, they suffer the same limitation.

We are here trying to apply the Barthian distinction between dogma and dogmas. We are trying to adopt Dr. Minear's distinction between the reality, and the images which men use to point to that reality. The result is that the coffee house ministry provides a place where the church can experience at least as much pluralism as Dr. Minear has shown is maintained by the canon. Can not the coffee house choose the same course? It only requires that our reliance is upon the reality of Jesus Christ, rather than any particular way of talking about him. It means that we accept and live with the limitations of all of our theological jargon. Earlier we spoke of the need to suppress sectarian symbols and ways of talking. Here we can add the other half of the coin—our sectarian ways of speaking can receive the same privileges that we permit and enable every other sectarian position. In short, we are trying to create a model of true pluralism in the coffee house.

The coffee house provides for the church a controlled experimental situation where we can demonstrate to the world, and to ourselves, the shape of authentic secularization. Our cherished religious position does not receive any special push. On the other hand, neither is it under any restraint, as frequently happens in the world. A good case in point is "Koinonia" coffee house at the University of Connecticut. On campus, religious views are seldom mentioned, and never given a forum. When "Koinonia" first opened, its leaders were afraid to mention religion. After many weeks of programming, the leaders reasoned that a "Christian" viewpoint had at least as much right to be heard as the variety of secularist viewpoints that were being presented by speakers and folk singers. The receptive response of audiences convinced the sponsors this was, in fact, a more accurate representation of pluralism.

It may in fact be that the atmosphere of acceptance based not upon human grounds but upon the reality of the activity of the incarnate and risen Lord is exactly what is meant by secularization. If the good news that Christ came to save all men means anything at all, it must mean that forgiveness and glorification are equally available to those of each theological school. If this is as true as it is biblical, the coffee house has the unique opportunity to function in the proclamation of *this good news,* by providing an equal forum for a variety of viewpoints. In this context, creativity, self-expression, stimulation, and dialogue take on a richer meaning. They are not arbitrary goals, but grow directly out of the reality of what God has done and is doing in the world.

All that is required is that someone serve in this humble capacity. The State cannot do it because it is always subject to criticism for being partisan, when one side or another comes off poorly. Commercial interests won't do it for fear of alienating the rest of the population. (Industry will sponsor programs at Christmas because it is a secular celebration; but they do not sponsor Easter programs!) And other agencies simply don't do it. It falls to the church alone to become this agent of reconciliation.

Program Content

A small percentage of the existing church-related coffee houses have no formal program at all. Some have no self-conscious "on stage" program, but use a "program" of conversation between the waiters and the customers. The coffee houses that operate this way justify their approach as a kind of "client-centered" relationship, in that whatever conversation develops grows out of the needs and cares that people bring in off the street with them. There may be some validity to this approach, if the waiters are properly trained.

Unfortunately, what people have on their minds when they come in off the street may not be very "deep," and it takes a long time for conversation with strangers to reach a significant level. Of course, conversations about apparently superficial things have been shown to be highly significant in terms of interpersonal relationships. The effect of programming content is to press more immediately into deep levels of discussion, in terms of content. But this may only be an egghead's view of significance. Content programs might, therefore, be more appropriate for educated audiences, such as on a college campus, where they might contribute to the overall educational process.

Among "content"-oriented coffee houses, all of the usual topics of discussion are live options. Programs common to all areas of student Christian movement activity, for instance, have been tried in the coffee house.

If we can distinguish between "religious" and "theological" program content, the latter certainly prevails. Very few coffee houses include overtly "religious" words, ideas, or symbols in their public programs. Most feel that the use of sectarian forms of communication should be confined to the in-group—the workers' training program, and traditional church activities.

They do make extensive use, however, of "theological" content in their programming. Activities which probe the "meaning of life," "ultimate questions," and the "genuinely human" are sought after and exploited. Such activities are found in music (both classical and folk, but seldom popular), poetry, drama, and the graphic arts (photography, painting, and sculpture). A few even go so far as to offer theological courses, usually in the form of small group discussions related to but not directly a part of the coffee house evening program.

A large number of coffee houses shun the overtly challenging kinds of program content, and insist instead upon "entertainment." It is important to note, however, that these "aficionados" operate with a view of "entertainment" which is defined by the traditions of serious theatre and art, and not from the "amusement" concept of entertainment typified in television programming today. The difference between "stimulating" programs and "entertainment" all but vanishes when we remember the definitions operating here.

There is no need to delineate any special types of coffee house programs to illustrate the "theological" approach of the coffee house ministry programs. One especially good source is the paper on "Ultimate Questions In Penultimate Form" by Harry E. Smith, published by U.C.C.F. Publications in St. Louis, Missouri. The campus work departments of almost all denominations have similar materials available.

Types of Coffee Houses

A noted educator completing a study of American higher education concluded that there are as many kinds of universities as there are universities. At first glance, this appears to be true also of coffee houses. But we can distinguish certain similarities on the basis of cultural location and age group served. There are five basic location types:

1. Resort area
2. College campus
3. Urban
4. Suburban
5. Inner-city

The *resort area* coffee house is a seasonal activity, usually set up temporarily in borrowed facilities to provide a special quality of recreation that would be otherwise missing. "The Church Key" in Yosemite National Park is a good example. It is run by Donald Baldwin, park chaplain, and a staff of student workers under the Christian Ministry in National Parks program of the National

Council of Churches. Every Tuesday and Friday night several hundred of Yosemite's 3,000 college student-workers flock to the redecorated Masonic Lodge to hear their peers—and the chaplain—sing folk songs and otherwise entertain. Before the coffee house was started, "beach parties" (consisting of beer, beaches, boys, and girls) were the workers' only social outlet. Similar coffee houses are in summer operation at other national parks. A group of enterprising Earlham College students, led by junior William Schlesinger got the Atlantic City Council of Churches and YWCA to jointly sponsor a store-front mission in that resort town. As the summer developed, "The Gallows" found a significant ministry in bringing interracial recreation and discussion to Atlantic City, New Jersey.

The majority of coffee houses are located on or near *college campuses*. They serve big institutions like the University of Pennsylvania, and small ones, like Johnson State College in Vermont. Some are operated almost every night of the week in rented storefronts or basements, while others exist for only a few short hours on Friday or Saturday evening. They share a common concern to provide a significant place for dating (to bring them or find them) and to contribute to the overall purposes of their universities through paracurricular programs and discussions. Historically, campus ministries began to think that when the university assumed greater responsibility for student recreation (in the Student Union movement) their own programs could shift away from recreation. It now seems, however, that there is still a need for campus ministries to provide certain kinds of facilities which the university is unable or unwilling to provide.

Most campus coffee houses, therefore, understand their role to include a contribution to the nominal and ideal purposes of the university. They react against the "objective" sterility of too much college teaching by providing a setting for the communication of values and feelings as supplements to "facts." Professors are invited to speak on what they feel strongly about, regardless of what the catalogue says they are teaching. An exchange of ideas and opinions is encouraged. We recall that one of Philip E. Jacob's conclusions in his study "Changing Values in College" was that teachers who have firmly held and openly expressed values, and share them in unhurried and informal conversation outside of class, have the greatest impact on student's values. A campus coffee house well run could conceivably have a greater effect on the values of its students than the rest of the university. Perhaps this is why a fair percentage of such coffee houses include deans of men on their controlling boards.

Urban coffee houses are urbane. From their plate glass windows looking out on the theater district through plush interiors to stainless steel kitchens in back, in obvious and external ways they resemble commercial restaurants. "The Potter's House" in Washington, D. C., is typical of a number of urban coffee houses in the larger cities. The most urbane provide little in the way of organized program, save perhaps a dramatic presentation once or twice a year. They are rather intended as gathering places for individuals and groups to come "after the show" down the street. Their "program" consists primarily of art exhibits on their walls, and intensified conversation between the waiters and customers.

A number of less sophisticated urban coffee houses, such as "The Encounter" in Lancaster, Pennsylvania, and "The Door" in Chicago make frequent use of formal "programs" and study-discussion groups. They even host lecture series and classes, often in conjunction with nearby seminaries. In this respect, they represent a hybrid version of the campus religious center combined with a lay academy for theological education. Because of their great success, we will undoubtably see many more of this type in the future.

Most *suburban* coffee houses are also urbane. They differ from their urban counterpart only in being located near residential areas, rather than in theatre districts. Sometimes they are located in small shopping centers, as is "The Vine and The Branch" of Claredon Hills, Chicago, but more often they use church facilities. The absence of old and therefore cheap accommodations in suburbia, together with abundant spacious ecclesiastical structures, might account for this shift. In cases where large numbers of teenagers are served, the suburban coffee house might be more like the following type.

Inner-city coffee houses are growing in number. In many

respects these teenage programs are glorified "teen canteens," but if that is true, then the change of name is a modern merchandising miracle, because they are fast growing in popularity. The "Chelsea Teen Coffee Shop" initiated by Barbara Fisher, Youth Director of St. Peter's Episcopal Church in New York City, under broad sponsorship, is a good example. It is, like most teen coffee houses, run by a committee of teenagers themselves, with adult supervision. While their menus are like other coffee houses, the atmosphere is, as one might expect, inclined to be noisier, and folk music is always in danger of being forced out by less sophisticated forms of instrumentation.

We must confess that the distinctions which we have thus set up look much more viable on paper than they do in reality. The very informality and flexibility of coffee house programs mediates against rigid stereotypes. A given coffee house may be one type on one night, and another on the next, depending upon who is running the program and who comes to it. To a certain extent selection of programs can control the appeal to one or another element, if formal programs are planned ahead of time. It would seem advisable to do so, since a public image (as, for instance, "a teenagers' place") will have a big effect on who comes. On the other hand, under certain circumstances a committee might wish to be flexible, to see who wants to come. When we open the doors wide, we are never quite sure who will accept our hospitality. This may be a blessing in our ministry.

Even more important than the actual content and form of the programs employed is the appropriateness of the program for the group involved. Many teenage coffee houses find that dancing contributes to their program goals, while adult coffee houses require more conversational programs. Teenage coffee house programs are usually "recreational" and continuous, adult programs formal and structured. Collegiate coffee house programs tend to be less formal, more spontaneous and flexible. Their conversations are less polite than the adult counterpart, more like bull session discussions. The wide differences in subcultures makes it difficult to predict appropriate programs for hypothetical audiences. But the selection of programs should always be the result of extensive wrestling with the needs of those to be served.

CONCLUSION

Our approach to the coffee house ministry has been essentially positive and constructive. We have not stressed the criticisms because it is a young movement which is barely begun. It would be unfortunate if this enthusiastic movement of the church toward the world of its own backyard were squashed by early pessimism. The preliminary evaluation of the movement has been that it is extremely promising, with at least three qualifications.

In the first place, the erection of a coffee house is no panacea. The mere institution of a coffee house program will not solve the problems of communicating the gospel in the modern world, any more than did Vatican II's declaration on the same subject. But hopefully, they are both steps in the right direction. The inception of coffee house ministry will only serve to crystallize and focus some of the fundamental problems involved. It will not solve them, but it will provide a means for experimentation, a vehicle to try out approaches to the post-Christian world. If the soul-searching, heartrending tensions of witnessing and proclaiming in our generation become more productive, the coffee house will earn a significant place in the history of the church.

In the second place, there is a danger that the coffee house ministry will become an escape route for the church. The coffee house is by its very nature a highly personalized form of ministry. It does not provide any opportunity for direct social and political action or involvement in the ongoing life of the church in the world, although these things can be effectively discussed there. If the coffee house ministry serves as an outlet for internal discussions of such affairs, it will be useful. But it must not become a trap for more talk and less action in the world.

The third qualification about the potential for the coffee house ministry has to do with the future. Some of the most vociferous "attacks" on coffee house ministry come from those who have been involved in it for a couple of years or more. In part they grow out of disillusionment with the limitations of the coffee house, but in part they grow out of an increasing sensitivity to the problems which the coffee house tries to meet.

In visiting coffee houses all over the country, we have sometimes perceived a lack of creative spark in many that have been living for three or four years, often with the same personnel. There are two characteristic responses to this challenge: either quiet acquiescence to the limitations of the coffee house ministry, or burning desire to move beyond it, without any real directions plotted yet.

In this matter, we can learn once again from the many creative insights of the Church of The Savior in Washington, D. C., founder of "The Potter's House." For them, "The Potter's House" is but one of many "mission" projects of the congregation. A member of that church characteristically spends two years in Christian education classes, and in the third year is "promoted" to participate in a mission project. But they have found it necessary to urge members to move on to new projects after a couple of years in one. The same pattern has emerged in churches which have developed small *koinonia* groups. After a year or two, it seems advisable for groups to split, and multiply.

If our present churches are as sedentary as the critics claim, our approach in the coffee house ministry perhaps ought not to be to found another new institution, but simply to make use of a timely pattern of ministry so long as it is helpful. This will surely mean that individuals ought to be "graduated" from the coffee house ministry after a couple of years' service. If volunteers (and clergymen) have learned anything about communication between peoples in their training in the coffee house, they may be prepared to venture into more "worldly" places, such as commercial coffee houses. There has already been a good deal of cross-fertilization between the commercial and church coffee houses through traveling folk singers who "drift" across the country. Where church-related coffee houses are truly "open" places, individuals who also patronize commercial coffee houses frequently come in. In any given community then, a volunteer who has met customers in the church coffee house will find that he can continue his friendship and conversation in other locations.

But we need to preserve some of the distinctive missionary emphases which we have been building. As coffee house volunteers "graduate" to taverns and bars, they will still need to be sent out "two by two." They will still require training for their mission. They will still be suffering servants, wherever they go. The calling of the Christian is essentially the same wherever he is. But the situations into which he is called change. Let us hope that the church will be aware of this. It may be that in a decade or two the church will be ready to undertake a tavern ministry. A few isolated individuals are already working on that, but apparently the church is not strong enough yet for it. On the other hand, perhaps the church is strong enough, but lacks the faith to dare. Some churches lack even the faith to venture as far into the world as the coffee house ministry. Thank God, He didn't.

Malcolm Boyd has objected that most church-related coffee houses appear to be only very slightly "in the world." They are often sterile, safe places of refuge, "less dirty" than the "real" coffee houses. In this evaluation, he is of course quite accurate. There are very few church-related coffee houses that appear ready to take on the whole world . . . just as there are very few churchmen that stand up (and get shot down) for the civil rights of their neighbors. But we are learning to show courage in the civil rights sphere, and, hopefully, we will learn something in the coffee house.

Some coffee house managers have become disillusioned about their operations. In a few cases this is because they lack the theological training to understand what is happening right under their noses. In others, it is because they had hoped for too much from the coffee house. Those who have really caught on to the latest "in-the-world" theology have a life-long calling to prepare their congregations for this ministry. Many Christians are caught between two alternatives: either to get out into the world themselves, or to stay in the church and help prepare it for ministry in the world. We began by noting the number of young clergymen who had elected the former. If the coffee house ministry has suggested that the latter alternative is both possible and, in the long run, infinitely more fruitful, then we have new cause to rejoice in the Mighty Acts of God.

La lune
La roux de fortune

SELECTED BIBLIOGRAPHY OF THE COFFEE HOUSE MOVEMENT

Anon. "Balaam's Ass Joins Campus Coffee Houses," *The Lutheran* (LCA), April 21, 1965, p. 35.

Anon. "Christian Coffee House Is Smash Hit in St. Louis," *The Lutheran* (LCA), February 10, 1965, p. 34; also printed in *Church and Home* (E.W.S.), March 15, 1965.

Anon. "Coffee Club Will Spread the Gospel," *Religious News Service,* August 25, 1965, p. 7 (news item on two fundamentalists' coffee houses in England; perhaps "club" rhymes better with "pub").

Anon. "Coffee House Theology in a Small Town," *The Lutheran* (LCA), January 13, 1965, p. 40.

Anon. "A Pastor-Poet Ministers to San Francisco's 'Beat Generation,'" *Presbyterian Life,* April 15, 1959, p. 23 (extensive discussion, with several photographs, of the "Bread and Wine Mission" of Pierre Dehattre).

Boyd, Malcolm. "And the Church Decided to Open a Coffee House . . . A Fable," *Intercollegian,* June 1965 (a satire on the frequent illusion that the church is "really" meeting the world in a church-controlled coffee house).

Boyd, Malcolm. "The Holy in Coffee Houses," *The Churchman,* October 1965, p. 10 (incisive critique of in-groupishness of church-sponsored coffee houses).

Bronnecke, Jack. "Glendale's Coffee House: An Experimental Witness at One Church of the Brethren in California," *The Messenger* of the Church of the Brethren, July 22, 1965, pp. 5-8 (discusses the "Brethren Coffee House," several photos).

Castle, David. "The Speckled Axe," *Friend's Journal, Quaker Thought and Life Today,* Vol. 11, No. 12, June 15, 1965, p. 315 (discusses this coffee house for teenagers in Indianapolis—history, purpose, etc.).

Dinwiddie, Sheila M. "Coffee, Anyone," *The Register-Leader* (Unitarian-Universalist Assoc.), Vol. 147, No. 8, October 1965, pp. 6ff. (brief introduction to the Unitarian coffee house in Norfolk, Virginia).

Doig, Carol M. "Preacher in Greasepaint," *Together* (Methodist Church),

July 1965, pp. 17-19 (discusses a coffee house run by a Cape Cod, Massachusetts, congregation in Eastham).

Dougherty, Charles T. "Christ by Gaslight," *National Catholic Magazine,* April 1965 (article on "The Exit" in St. Louis).

Fackre, Gabriel J. "Encounter—Mission in the World," *International Journal of Religious Education,* October 1964, pp. 6, 7, 38 (a longer essay on "The Encounter" coffee house, including three photos).

Fackre, Gabriel J. "Lancaster Churches Sponsor Lay Center," *Christian Community* (UCC), Vol. 16, No. 4, December 1963, p. 1 (summary of "The Encounter" coffee house in early stages, one photo).

Franz, Delton. "Preaching in the Marketplace," *The Mennonite,* November 28, 1961, pp. 756f. (describes "The Quiet Place" in Chicago, two photographs).

Furlow, Frances. "Lives Are Changed in This Famous Congregation," *Presbyterian Survey,* November 1963, pp. 18-21 (describes in detail the Church of The Savior, in Washington, D. C., and its coffee house, "The Potter's House," two photos).

Hawthorne, Robert J. "Intersection: Point of Meeting," *The Christian Century,* December 29, 1965, pp. 1599ff. (a "breakthrough" series article on this comprehensive program which includes a coffee house).

Hollister, William H. "The Church 'out there': How can the Church be a people faithful to Jesus Christ?" *International Journal of Religious Education,* September 1965, pp. 4-5, 39 (describes the activities of a freewheeling Presbyterian congregation, including "The Loft" coffee house and bookstore, two photos).

Huldschiner, Robert E. "Students Are People," *The Lutheran* (LCA), April 24, 1963, p. 6.

Muller, Carol A. "Engaging the City with Love," *Together* (Methodist Church), May 1965, pp. 14-18 (discusses the activities of the Glide Foundation in San Francisco, including "The Precarious Vision," which now has merged into the "Intersection").

McDonald, Carol. "The Exit," *Presbyterian Survey,* August 1965, pp. 24-25 (describes this rather exciting "Christian Coffee House" in St. Louis' Gaslight district, two photos).

O'Conner, Elizabeth. *The Call to Commitment,* Harper & Row, 1963 (a book dealing with the life and mission of the Church of The Savior, in Washington, D. C., including a chapter on "The Potter's House").

Perry, John D. "The Coffee House Ministry: Special Report," *The Christian Century,* February 10, 1965, p. 180 (describes the now out-of-print original survey of the coffee house movement).

Perry, John D. "The Coffee House: Evangelism or Evasion?" *motive,* March 1965, Vol. 25, No. 6, p. 10 (an attempt to stimulate theological discussion about the coffee house ministry, eight photos).

Reqier, Marie. "Visitors to the Quiet Place," *The Mennonite,* November 16, 1965, pp. 712-713 (some recent experiences at "The Quiet Place" in Chicago).

Southwick, William. "The Door," *Concern* (United Presbyterian Women), September 1965, Vol. 7, No. 7 (one-page article describing this coffee house and bookstore in Chicago, by its manager).

Strunkel, O. "The Gaslight Gospel," *This Day* (Concordia Publishing House), May 1965 (article on "The Exit" in St. Louis).

Wavrinek, Owen. "Open Doors and Open Minds," *The National Lutheran* (National Lutheran Council), April 1965, pp. 4-5 (discusses in detail "The Unmuzzled Ox" at Ithaca, including three photos, by a student).

Coffee Syrup
(Coffee Information Service)

Viennese Velvet
(Pan-American Coffee Bureau)

Turkish Coffee
(Pan-American Coffee Bureau)

APPENDIX

COFFEE RECIPES

Coffee House Coffee

Regular fresh-ground, fresh-brewed coffee can be made in a big coffee pot, an urn, or an electric percolator.

Here is a rule of thumb for three strengths of coffee: for recommended strength, 1 part ground coffee, 6 parts water; moderate strength, 1 part ground coffee, 7 parts water; light strength, 1 part ground coffee, 8 parts water.

The chart below shows the exact proportion of coffee and water for 6, 8, and 12 servings of Coffee House Coffee.

	6 Servings	*8 Servings*	*12 Servings*
Recommended	6 standard measures ground coffee to 4½ cups water	8 standard measures ground coffee to 6 cups water	12 standard measures ground coffee to 9 cups water
Moderate	5 standard measures ground coffee to 4½ cups water	7 standard measures ground coffee to 6 cups water	10 standard measures ground coffee to 9 cups water
Light	4½ standard measures ground coffee to 4½ cups water	6 standard measures ground coffee to 6 cups water	9 standard measures ground coffee to 9 cups water

Note: a "standard measure" is 2 level measuring tablespoonfuls—a "cup" means one standard measuring cup or 8 ounces—a "serving" means an average cup of coffee or 5½ ounces of liquid.

Keep the coffee pot clean, since coffee leaves an invisible oil inside the pot which affects the flavor of the next batch.

Never allow brewed coffee to come to a boil. Boiling ruins the flavor of coffee. If the coffee boils, discard it and start over.

Serve coffee piping hot. Keep freshly brewed coffee at serving temperature over very low heat.

Instant Coffee

Properly prepared, instant coffee served from a heat-proof carafe can be delicious, too. It also has several advantages:

1. It is easily made by merely mixing instant coffee powder and boiling water.
2. Because there are no coffee grounds, cleaning up is easy.
3. The strength of the coffee is easily adjusted by adding more coffee powder or more boiling water.
4. Instant coffee is available in espresso as well as the regular kind.

Instant coffee should never be held at serving temperature more than ten to fifteen minutes. The coffee powder should be thoroughly dissolved in a small amount of hot water first. Then measured boiling water can be added or the coffee solution can be added to measured hot water. Coffee powder should not be added directly to water in the pot, as this causes foaming and frothing. Make instant coffee in small quantities and have less waste.

To prepare instant coffee, use:

1. Heat-proof glass servers from one quart to a quart-and-a-half capacity.
2. A reliable hot-plate with graduated heating controls so it can heat water or keep coffee at serving temperature.
3. A kettle for heating water—one which pours easily.
4. Heat-proof glass measuring cups—1-cup, 2-cup, 4-cup.

The average strength for a single serving of instant coffee is 1 rounded teaspoon of coffee powder to ¾ measuring cup of water.

To make larger amounts of instant coffee, measure the coffee powder into a heat-proof server. Dissolve the powder in a little boiling water and then add a measured quantity of boiling water. Stir and serve.

Here are proportions for more servings: For 5 servings use ¼ cup instant coffee and 1 quart water; for 11 servings use ½ cup instant coffee and 2 quarts water; for 23 servings use 1 measuring cup instant coffee (2 oz. jar) and 1 gallon water.

Cool Coffees

Some of the following recipes must be made in the electric blender—others can be whipped with a rotary beater or whisk. All are easy to make, good to look at, and well worth the extra effort.

Coffee Hula is made by combining 2 cups strong cold coffee, 1 cup chilled pineapple juice, and 1 pint soft coffee ice cream. Beat with a beater or in an electric blender until the mixture is smooth and foamy. Pour into four big, tall glasses.

Coffee Nova is made with 1½ cups strong cooled coffee and one tablespoon granulated sugar. Fill the electric blender container half full of ice (preferably finely chopped). Add the coffee and sugar. Blend until thick and foamy. Pour into four tall glasses and serve.

Coffee Coola is easy to make. Fill tall glasses with ice and pour in double-strength coffee, filling glasses ⅓ full. Add cola, filling glasses to the top. Garnish with twists of lemon peel.

Coffee Cream is a frothy, creamy, fizz drink made by combining in a bowl or pitcher 2 cups strong cold coffee, ½ teaspoon bitters, and ½ cup heavy cream. Divide among four tall glasses. Fill glass to top with chilled cream soda. Stir gently to mix.

MORE COFFEE RECIPES

Spiced Coffee Vienna

- 3 cups hot, extra-strength coffee
- 2 cinnamon sticks
- 4 whole cloves
- 4 allspice berries
- whipped cream for topping
- nutmeg

Pour very hot coffee over the cinnamon sticks, cloves, and allspice berries. Let stand over lowest heat for 10 to 15 minutes. Strain.

Pour into table wine glasses and top with softly whipped cream. Sprinkle with nutmeg and serve with sugar. Makes 6 servings.

Creamed Cinnamon Coffee

4 cups strong, hot coffee
3 sticks cinnamon
sugar or sugar syrup
½ cup heavy cream

Pour hot coffee over cinnamon sticks and let stand for about one hour. Remove cinnamon sticks and sweeten coffee to taste. Add heavy cream and chill. Pour over cracked ice in tall glasses and use cinnamon sticks as stirrers. Makes 4 to 5 servings.

Viennese Velvet

1 quart vanilla ice cream
6 cups hot, double-strength coffee
whipped cream

Place one large scoop of vanilla ice cream in each of six tall glasses. Pour hot, double-strength coffee carefully over ice cream until glass is about ⅔ full. Add a second scoop of ice cream and fill glass with coffee. Garnish with whipped cream, and add a sprinkle of nutmeg if desired.

Turkish Coffee

1½ measuring cups water
6 tablespoons finely ground coffee
3 tablespoons sugar

Measure sugar and coffee into a heavy saucepan or an "Ibrik." Stir over heat until it comes to a boil and is frothy. Remove from heat until froth subsides. Return to heat and repeat process twice more, three times in all. Before serving, add a few drops of cold water to settle grounds. Spoon some of foam into demitasse cups and pour coffee. Makes 4 demitasse servings. Pulverized regular coffee is best for Turkish Coffee. A few drops of rose water may be added. Cream is never used with Turkish Coffee.

Spiced Coffee Vienna
(Pan-American Coffee Bureau)

Creamed Cinnamon Coffee
(Pan-American Coffee Bureau)

Caffe Borgia
(Coffee Information Service)

Caffe Cappuccino
(Coffee Information Service)

Caffe Borgia

Combine equal quantities of steaming coffee and hot chocolate. (Both can be made with instant products if you prefer.) Pour into cups and top with sweetened whipped cream. Sprinkle with grated orange peel.

Coffee Syrup

- 4 tablespoons instant coffee powder
- ½ cup hot water
- ¼ teaspoon ground cinnamon
- ½ teaspoon nutmeg
- 2 cups light corn syrup
- ⅛ teaspoon salt
- 2 teaspoons vanilla

Dissolve coffee in hot water. Stir in remaining ingredients except vanilla. Bring to boil, lower heat, and simmer for 5 minutes. Remove from heat, skim, and cool. Stir in vanilla. Store in covered jar in refrigerator. Yield: about 2¼ cups. Coffee syrup is poured over vanilla, coffee, or chocolate ice cream. Serve with espresso coffee containing lemon peel and sugar.

Caffe Cappuccino

Make desired quantity of steaming Italian coffee. (An easy way to make it is by using espresso instant coffee.) Combine coffee with equal quantity of steaming milk. Pour into Cappuccino cups and sprinkle with cinnamon or nutmeg. Serve with sugar and a stick of cinnamon as stirrer.

PHOTO CREDITS

p. 18—Two students, summer workers, take time off to relax at "The Church Key," a summer coffee house for workers at Yosemite National Park. (John D. Perry, Jr.)

Chapter 1

p. 22—A door becomes a blackboard at "The Door" Coffee House in Chicago. Their extensive collateral programming is hinted at in this listing. (Chicago Sun-Times)

p. 30—Music is not the only entertainment in coffee houses. Here a student reads poetry to an obviously interested audience. (Des Moines Tribune and Register)

Chapter 2

p. 32—Two lady shoppers talk with a waiter at the attractive "Golden Lamp," in Burlingame, California. (John D. Perry, Jr.)

p. 40—A Greek play is presented at the Y's coffee house, "The Way?" in Chicago. (John D. Perry, Jr.)

Chapter 3

p. 42—Miss Jean Murray interviews the author for Channel Two, New York City TV, on the release of the Coffee House Study Project report in 1965. (Coffee Information Service)

Chapter 4

p. 52—Bright lights and a clear view invite the stranger through "The Door" in Chicago. (Chicago Sun-Times)

p. 59—All ages gather for conversation at "The Sign of the Tarot" in Denver. A group of six clergymen pooled their resources when this fine coffee house failed commercially. (John D. Perry, Jr.)

Chapter 5

p. 60—"Victoria," an ancient and troublesome espresso machine, dominates the decor of "The Sign of the Tarot." (John D. Perry, Jr.)

p. 66—A waitress prepares cold drinks in the crowded kitchen of "The Center," in Jackson, Wyoming. (John D. Perry, Jr.)

Chapter 6

p. 68—Customers frequently use the coffee house for creative stimulation—writing poetry, for instance. Some coffee houses make a point to provide paper and pencils at every table. (Chicago Sun-Times)

p. 73—Folk music, played on a variety of instruments in addition to the traditional guitar, is still the most common form of entertainment in coffee houses. (Coffee Information Service)

Chapter 7

p. 76—Seminarian-Manager chats with a customer at Yellowstone National Park (summertime) Coffee House while an electric guitar booms in the background. (John D. Perry, Jr.)

p. 84—A waitress refills cups during a performance at the "Brethren Coffee House" in Glendale, California. (Coffee Information Service)

p. 92—"Intersection" Coffee House in San Francisco features the "bar and bartender" type ministry shown here. (John D. Perry, Jr.)

Chapter 9

p. 94—Malcolm Boyd performs in one of his controversial plays on racial prejudice, in "Laissez Faire," a Daytona Beach coffee house. (Malcolm Boyd)

Conclusion

p. 108—Simplicity in equipment can be attractive. This inexpensive brown mug is frequently seen. (Chicago Sun-Times)

Bibliography

p. 114—Giant "tarot card" panels carry out the theme and decorate the walls of "The Sign of the Tarot" Coffee House in Denver. (John D. Perry, Jr.)